CW00403505

Tales of a Lakeland Valley

BORROWDALE

**based on collected memories, stories and
information about the Lakeland valley**

by

Sheila Richardson

additional research by B. S. Richardson

**Some of the stories
have needed a little help on the part of the author,
to enlarge a collection of mere facts into a readable tale.**

Published by Mill Field Publications - Printed by Derwent Press, Workington

Tales of a Lakeland Valley - BORROWDALE

British Library Cataloguing in Publication Data. A catalogue record for this book is
available from the British Library
ISBN 0 9526665 1 0

Cover photographs show two pack horse bridges;
Ashness Bridge (front) and Watendlath Bridge (back)

View looking up Derwentwater into Borrowdale

Mill Field Publications, 8 Everest Mt., Workington, Cumbria, CA14 5BY;
01900 602216

CONTENTS

By the same author

A Lakes Christmas
Tales of a Lakeland Poacher
Tales of a Lakeland Valley - Buttermere
Tales of a Lakeland Gypsy [in preparation]

It would have been impossible to produce this book without the help of the following;

    The Staff of the County Records Office, Carlisle
    Victor Brownlee, Stonethwaite Farm
    Dick Richardson, Fold Head Farm, Watendlath
    David Tyson, Stepps Farm, Watendlath
    Stan Edmondson, Seathwaite Farm
    Richard Brownrigg, Keswick
    Mrs Margaret Horsley, Rosthwaite
    Alan Mounsey, Grange in Borrowdale
    Kenneth Robinson, Troutdale
    Mr and Mrs Willie Hind, Stonethwaite
    Mike Roulson, Stonethwaite.
    David Thomason, Keswick
    Tommy Richardson, Keswick

My thanks and appreciation are due to those who were so generous with their time and information.

CHAPTER ONE

Introducing Borrowdale

Sheltered by Skiddaw to the north, flanked to the west and east by a continuous extension of mountainous arms, and ending to the south with the mass of Great End and its attendant mountains, Borrowdale could arguably be described as the most complete mountain valley.

Or should it be better described as a complexity of valleys, for the hanging valley of Watendlath, the quiet and retreating side valley of Troutdale, and the aptly named Langstrath, all add variety and interest to the main valley, to which they adjoin, or overlook. An early visitor to the valley who is recorded in William Gilpin's Observations on Lakes and Mountains written in 1772 , described Borrowdale as *"Beauty lying in the lap of Horreur."*

Borrowdale was formed millions of years ago as part of a time scale incomprehensible to most, when the melting glaciers of the Ice Age gouged their ways through the igneous rock of the mountains of the central Lake District. Indeed, Borrowdale volcanic is the name by which this type of rock is known to geologists, and its rugged outlines of summits and ridges, contrast with the smoother slopes of the very much older Skiddaw slates to the north.

The name Borrowdale is thought to originate from the Norse language, for in the records of Furness Abbey, to whom much of the valley once belonged, it is written as Borcherdale, which means the valley of the fort. Others claim the name derives from "borga", the term for a wild boar.

Castle Crag, which stands in a dominant position as one of the Jaws of Borrowdale, was almost certainly the site of a stronghold at many different periods of its history. The names of some of the hamlets also indicates a strong Norse influence. "Thwaite" is a Norse word meaning a clearing, and Stonethwaite, Longthwaite and Rosthwaite are three examples of settlements alongside the river Derwent that flows through the valley. From other place names, such as Glaramara, and the name of the river Derwent itself, there is evidence to suggest that there were Celtic people living in the valley. Going further back in time, relics of stone age settlement was discovered in 1901, when a pond was dug at Portinscale. Remains were found under the soil that were thought to be those of an abandoned axe workshop. Evidence of this was in the half worked stones and chippings from axe heads left lying there. One wonders if there was an association between those early inhabitants of Portinscale and the circle of stones that stands so majestically at Castlerigg high above Keswick.

There is easy access by road into Borrowdale, but this was not always so. William Gilpin, a cleric who visited the valley as early as 1752 wrote, *"On the 9th June we set out*

Tales of a Lakeland Valley - BORROWDALE

on horse - back, (which I mention, as it is the only conveyance the road will admit) on an expedition into Borrodale; a wild country south west of Keswick"

The modern road into Borrowdale leaves Keswick at the Moot Hall, a 19th century building which was erected on the site of a former jail. At one time it was a market hall. and now is the Tourist Information Office. The route to be followed into Borrowdale winds through narrow streets before emerging on the brow of a hill where one gains the first view of the valley that extends right into the heart of the Lake District. Fields and pockets of woodland, craggy fell sides and a silvered lake fill the foreground, while in the blued distance, the projection of rock called Castle Crag seems to block any further route south. On closer acquaintance, a good, if narrow road winds below Castle Crag to follow a confined way along the east side of the river Derwent. The valley then opens out into a wide and pleasant strath of pasture land with hamlets and farms. This is the area that includes what Alfred Wainwright, noted for his Lake District guide books, describes as the loveliest square mile in Lakeland.

"No high mountain, no lake, no famous crag, no tarn. But, in the author's humble submission, it encloses the loveliest square mile in Lakeland - the Jaws of Borrowdale."

The hamlet of Rosthwaite lies to the south of the Jaws and from there fingers of lesser valleys span out. Greenup leads over the fell to Grasmere, Langstrath climbs over the Stake to Langdale, while the craggy arms of Rosthwaite Fell and Thornythwaite Fell open up to allow access alongside Coombe Beck. The extremity of Borrowdale is Seathwaite, the name is a modern corruption of its former name of Satterthwaite, where tracks lead one into the heart of the Lake District by the mountain passes of Sty Head and Grains Gill. At Seatoller, motor bound visitors can leave Borrowdale for Buttermere by climbing the steep gradients of the road over Honister Pass.

The remains of a much rougher road follows the west side of the river Derwent from Grange in Borrowdale. This former miners' and pack horse route climbs between Castle Crag and Scawdale, from where a turn to the west gives access to the Dale Head quarries, while a continuation along the road allows the summit of Honister Hause to be reached in a relatively easy manner.

The lake of the valley is Derwentwater, which is about three miles long and over a mile wide, and was a favourite haunt of the children's' writer, Beatrix Potter who used to spend the long summer months with her family in one of the large houses that were built close to the lake side. She recorded in her journal that *"the Keswick toughs have a habit of getting drunk on a Saturday night, "*and subsequently falling into the lake. *"One hardly likes to go up the lake with such things under the water. They ruin the lake for boating."* In spite of her misgivings, Borrowdale and its lake provide the settings for a number of illustrations in her books.

Boating is today a very popular activity on the lake. The needs of local people and visitors are accommodated with a private sailing club, launches, and rowing and motor boats that are available for members of the public to hire. The lake is rich in fish and bird life, with perch and pike making an ample food supply for the large number of heron, cormorant, mergansers and goosanders. Permits for fishing may be obtained in Keswick.

The lake is rarely calm for lengthy periods, which give good conditions for sailing and windsurfing, while the strong currents created by the river making its way through the lake give canoeists an easy ride from south to north, but a more difficult passage when travelling in the opposite direction. The up draught of winds from the valley also encourage hang gliders and para gliders to launch themselves from the valley ridges to float like colourful birds above the valley scene.

The valley has vastly changed in character, especially over the last three hundred years. Where there are now grassy slopes on the fells, these were formerly covered with dense woodland of oak, rowan, birch, holly and hazel. Much of that timber was felled for early industrial charcoal, while the increase in sheep farming has prevented much regeneration of natural woodland. Even as long ago as 1793, the human population of Borrowdale was recorded as being 361, while the number of sheep exceeded 9,000. But sufficient trees remain for the spectacular show of autumn colour. The Borrowdale birches are renowned for their brilliance as the lower fell sides become bathed in the gold of their changing leaves. The bronze of bracken vies with the richness of the beech leaf canopy, while the flush of rowan and holly berries provides not only a gaudy show, but a tempting food store for many wintering birds.

Borrowdale is rich in bird species. This was reputed to be the last nesting place of the sea eagle in Britain before its re-introduction to the Scottish western islands. A study of an ordnance map of the valley and the surrounding area indicates the many Eagle or Erne [sea eagle] Crags. While the eagle may now be missing from the valley, the spectacular peregrine is commonly seen. The agitated scream of the bird can be heard almost all the year round. The wardening of sites, and the co-operation of climbers in avoiding nesting crags has done much to ensure a remarkable recovery of these once threatened birds. One of the easiest sites at which to observe peregrines is from the Borrowdale road, below the appropriately named Falcon Crag.

The remaining stands of oak woodlands provide the ideal habitat for many different species of birds, nest box schemes have encouraged the increase of numbers of pied fly catchers, the nuthatch has become relatively common, while the rich food supply of the lake ensures its attraction for many different water birds.

It has to be admitted that motorists find that parking can be a problem in Borrowdale. In relation to the number of visitors who visit the valley at busy times of the year, there are relatively few parking spaces. It pays to come early, for the National Trust car parks rapidly fill up. The alternative way to explore the valley is to leave the car in Keswick, and use one of the bus, mini coach or launch services that operate a regular timetable. In this way, one can travel in relative comfort, and give one's full attention to appreciate the splendour of what many would feel to be the most beautiful valley in the Lake District.

Before personal transport was so easily affordable, the weekend journeys of the "Borrowdale Bus", were adventures in the company of some of the local bus drivers. A number of the drivers boasted that they never left anyone at a bus stop. No matter how many were already packed on the bus, there always seemed to find room for more. "Pack in tight, "one would shout, "Git like spoons, yan on top of another." It was impossible to extract money from a pocket, or in some cases get off at the correct stop. But no one cheated, no one grumbled if they missed their stop, and if a weary walker was seen on the road, there was a good chance the bus would stop.

Memories of Borrowdale, of even forty years ago, bring back images of a slower pace of life. There were characters to chat to, rocks to climb, and caves of the slate quarries to explore. Rucksacks could be left at the foot of a crag, or beside a bridge to be collected later knowing the contents would be still intact and undamaged. At the end of a long day on the fells, there was the welcoming sight of farm house tables groaning with food. The weather was much the same; on not infrequent occasions it rained torrents, at other times the sun blazed hotly down. There were fish in the becks and fruit on the hedgerows. You could pitch a tent in a wood, alongside a stream, or on the fell without legislative restrictions. There was time to appreciate the valley.

Now a new school has replaced the old Victorian building. Camp sites have emerged and convenience type food enables many catering establishments to provide a greater variety of menu than the traditional ham and eggs. But take a look at the dates on some of the cottages 1689, 1745, and think of some of the events their silent windows must have witnessed.

This book is an attempt to bring to life some of the memories and stories of a still living valley that is visited every year by people from all over the world. It holds a wealth of attractions for all its visitors. The variety of landscape, of fell, farm, and lake means it has something of interest for everyone.

It is impossible to be bored in Borrowdale.

Walkers on Maiden Moor pause to admire the view into Borrowdale

CHAPTER TWO

The Memory Trail

When people visit an area, especially for the first time, they often like to follow a planned route in order to become familiar with their surroundings. This Memory Trail is a route with a difference, for the aim is to complete a circular tour of Derwentwater and visit memorials, or places that held great significance to some of the famous and not so famous people who loved the valley of Borrowdale and its lake.

The journey can be made by car or cycle, or by using a combination of the valley bus service, a launch trip and a short amount of walking. Hardier souls may prefer to undertake the whole of the trail on foot. But however the journey is made, the knowledge that present day visitors are seeking out reminders of others who loved the valley, ensures a feeling of companionship, especially to the solo traveller. Throughout the trail, the scenery is spectacular.

The early guide book writer, Thomas West suggested the use of the term "Stations" from which to view some of the most beautiful scenery in the Lake District. Our Stations will not be only vantage points, but will be the sites where specific memorials can be located on the journey.

Let's begin by leaving Keswick to head for the lake.

Station 1 is to be found about half a mile along the raised path that leads from the boat landing stages at Derwentwater. Just a little way past Derwent Island Cottage, there is a memorial stone set into the wall. This is dedicated to the memory of Canon Rawnsley, who was for many years Vicar of Crosthwaite. He was one of the great champions of the Lake District; he wrote letters to the national press if part of it was under threat; he organised petitions against developers; in short, he was a vigilant watch-dog for the area. Had he been alive today, no doubt he would have played a leading role in such organisations as friends of the Lake District, Friends of the Earth, the Cumbrian Wildlife Trust, and any other organisation that was concerned with the conservation of landscape and nature. As it was, he was one of the co - founders of the National Trust.

He was a prolific writer of Lake District books, and although his style may be too romantic for many, he realised the importance of recording information about the area as it was, and included stories given to him by local people. He was also a long time, and close friend of Beatrix Potter; and had it not been for Canon Rawnsley's encouragement, Peter Rabbit and Squirrel Nutkin may have sunk into oblivion before they were introduced to a wider readership. Rawnsley recognised her artistic talents, and persuaded her to persevere with her writing and drawings through publishing her own work after it had been initially rejected by a publishing house.

Even his name, Hardwicke Drummond Rawnsley has a grand ring to it; as sturdy and dependable sounding as the names of the fells themselves. It is fitting that his memorial, which is inscribed on green slate, is set firm and square in a place of prominence on the path to Friars Crag.

Many pass it by without a second look, but it is worth spending a brief moment to read the words and ponder on the man.

TO THE HONOURED MEMORY OF
HARDWICKE DRUMMOND RAWNSLEY 1851 - 1920
WHO GREATLY LOVED THE FAIR THINGS OF NATURE AND ART
HE WAS CANON OF CARLISLE CHAPLAIN TO THE KING
VICAR OF CROSTHWAITE 1883 - 1917 AND ONE OF THE FOUNDERS
OF THE NATIONAL TRUST INTO WHOSE CARE FRIARS CRAG
LORDS ISLAND AND A PART OF GREAT WOOD WERE GIVEN
BY SUBSCRIBERS WHO DESIRE THAT HIS NAME
SHOULD NOT BE FORGOTTEN 7 SEPTEMBER 1922

Station 2 is only a little further from the Rawnsley memorial and can be found by following the path to the well known beauty spot of Friars' Crag. Here is an imposing memorial of Borrowdale stone erected to the memory of the writer, artist, scholar, philosopher, mineralogist, social reformer and philanthropist, John Ruskin who first came to the lakes as a child in 1824. This early visit aroused a love for the Lake District which lasted for the rest of his life. The memorial was unveiled on the cloudy and stormy 6th October in 1900 and bears the words,

"The first thing which I remember as an event in my life, was being taken by my nurse to the brow of Friars Crag on Derwentwater."

In many peoples' minds, Ruskin has a closer affinity with Coniston, the area in which he spent a considerable part of his life, but the view from Friars' Crag looking down into Borrowdale provided him with one of his earliest memories as the words on the memorial explain. It was also, in his opinion as a much travelled man, one of the three most beautiful views in Europe.

The unveiling of the memorial is graphically described by Canon Rawnsley who was a great admirer of "the Professor", and is documented in Rawnsley's own book "Ruskin and the English Lakes."

"The monument in its simplicity and sincerity has at any rate the merit of telling its own story and of being devoid of any unnecessary ornament. It is of the stone of the country, and placed here on this grassy knoll among the trees, seems to be a natural part of the surroundings..."

The grassy knoll is now somewhat worn, and intermeshed with tree roots, but the view from the spot is virtually unaltered and still magnificent.

Station 3. This next memorial can be found by travelling south along the valley road, or wandering along the lake shore, until the narrow junction to Watendlath leaves the main valley road. A steep pull up the hill that leads to Ashness Bridge can leave the walker gasping for breath, but this is the most fitting way to approach this third memorial which is dedicated to the memory of Bob Graham.

"In memory of Bob Graham 1889 - 1966
of Keswick who on the 13 - 14 June 1932
traversed 42 Lakeland Peaks within 24 hours.
A record which stood for 28 years."

Bob Graham was a Borrowdale guest house owner, and an accomplished mountaineer. From the latter years of the 19th century, when men were beginning to challenge the rocks and heights of the Lake District mountains, some wanted to achieve more that attaining the height of a single mountain. They set themselves a personal challenge of fitness, navigation and achievement by attempting to reach as many Lake District summits as possible within a twenty four hour period. Among them were such Lake District legends as W.T Palmer, Eustace Thomas and other early members of the Fell and Rock Climbing Club of the English Lake District. They covered awesome distances on foot, many well in excess of 75 miles within the time set.. When Bob Graham eclipsed their successes in 1932, by attaining 42 summits, it was felt that his target would be impossible to better; and so it proved for the next 28 years. Since then, the "Bob Graham Round," as it has come to be known, has attracted such interest that there is now a Bob Graham Club, membership of which is only open to those who successfully complete the challenge.

Station 4. If one travels down the Borrowdale valley by car, it is very easy to miss this next station, for it is a stone seat that is set high on the bank above the river Derwent. It is not so much a memorial, as a place to sit and rest. However, a small car park gives the opportunity to leave the car and cross the road to take advantage of the seat. Pedestrians who make the long walk down the valley have even more cause to be grateful to the donor, for it has been welcomed by many a tired walker making the journey either north or south.

The location of the site may seem something of a puzzle, for the inscription on the seat bears tribute to the beautiful view that it was once possible to see when looking down the river towards the village of Grange in Borrowdale. What needs to be remembered however, is that in the intervening years between the erection of the seat, and modern travellers taking advantage of its location, scrub willow, bramble and hazel have sprung up on the river bank and now almost obliterate the view of the village, with its twin spanned bridge.

Nevertheless, it is still a pleasant spot to rest for a few minutes on a warm sunny day, to enjoy the bird song, maybe catch a glimpse of a red squirrel, or be startled by the "cronk" of a heron before continuing one's journey refreshed by the sights and sounds of a Lakeland day.

The inscription on the seat which was repaired by the National Trust in 1912 , are words written by HDR, the initials of Hardwicke Drummond Rawnsley

"Here travellers rest and feel the potent charm
Of fell and valley, bridge and clustered farm.
Make them thine own, no absence shall destroy
The hamlet's peace - the ancient river's joy."

Station 5. This next station can also be easily missed by speeding motorists, but the roadside well about a quarter of a mile south of Grange, was once a most welcome sight and place of refreshment when valley travel was a good deal more leisurely than it is today. This particular memorial is dedicated to W Hodgson, and is inscribed.

> **"He prayeth well who loveth well**
> **Both man and bird and beast."**
> **For the dear God who loveth us,**
> **He made and loveth all.**
> **September 1878**

William Hodgson died on 18th September 1878, when he was only 18. The cause of his death was consumption. He was the son of Thomas Hodgson of Keswick, and his death cut short his promising talent as an artist. In 1876 he became a student at Lambeth Art School. A fellow student described him as "little more than a boy from Keswick; full of enthusiasm and with an innermost touch of genius." It is said that he was proficient with the pencil before he could either walk or talk, and had a great gift for capturing the character of any man or animal that he drew.

His memorial stone of green slate stands above a roadside trough that always seems to be brimful of crisp, clean water, although in severe winters it can be found encased in ice. One can imagine how much it was appreciated by those who travelled the rough valley track on foot, or by horse, before the days of mechanical transport.

Among them would be the packman, who took the opportunity to pause there for a few moments with his black fell pony. His load of pots and pans, cottons and cloth, ribbons and bows brought extra colour and sound to the valley as he made his way to call at remote farmsteads. He was always made welcome to sell some of his wares and accept a bite of food and possibly a jug of ale from the hospitable valley folk. In return he would pass on items of gossip that he had gleaned from other farms, and in this way, circulate the news of the valley and its people.

Station 6. To reach this next station, it is necessary to retrace one's steps from the trough, and return to Grange; there to cross over the twin arches of the bridge. The area around Grange was formerly owned by the monks of Furness Abbey and it was here that their tithes of corn were stored. It is recorded in William Gilpin's Observations on the Lakes made in 1772 that, *"...they amassed here the valuable minerals of the country ; among which, salt, produced from a spring in the valley, was no inconsiderable article."* If the road is followed through the village, a stone building is reached on the first sharp bend of the road as it turns towards Manesty . The following memorial is set into what appears to have been a window space. **"This school was erected to the memory of Miss Margaret Heathcote mainly by the subscription of personal friends and others who thus recognised a life of good works spent among and for the inhabitants of the neighbourhood. The first stone was laid October 4 1894 by Miss Langton of Barrow House."** The school closed in 1932 due to falling numbers, when the children were transferred to the "big school" at Stonethwaite.

Miss Heathcote, who was " a lady of strong ideas," financed the building of a small church at Grange in 1860. It is built of green slate and in the external walls can be seen tiny chippings which Miss Heathcote pushed into the cracks between the stones. Inside, there are striking dog toothed decorative arches that span the church, and act as a reminder of the early form of architectural decoration used by Norman builders. Among other good works that Margaret Heathcote did for the local inhabitants, was to set up a private school in her own home, which is now better known as the Borrowdale Gates Hotel. The children gathered, in what is now, room number five of the Hotel, to learn their letters, to spell, calculate, and to read and write. Miss Heathcote was a stern, but kindly lady, who was only prepared to stand so much nonsense from some of her more mischievous charges. On one occasion, when a young girl called Polly had just tried Miss Heathcote's patience too much, punishment was meted out. Miss Heathcote decided to detain Polly, and locked the child in another upstairs room. When lunch time came, Miss Heathcote visited Polly's home to warn her mother that her daughter would be late. She was greatly surprised to find that Polly was already there and heartily enjoying her dinner. Miss Heathcote was even more surprised to learn that Polly had made her escape from her upstairs room by climbing out of the window and sliding down the slanting slate of the porch roof. Suffice to say, Polly received punishment twice over...

Station 7. Continue along the road that rises high above Derwentwater until the house called Brackenburn is reached. Walkers may prefer to wander through the woods, and join the road above the launch jetty.

Brackenburn was a former bungalow that was converted into a house for Sir Hugh Walpole, and it remained his home for many years. Although he was a prolific writer, much of his fame is due to the creation of his four volume series, "The Herries Chronicles", which is set in Borrowdale and other parts of the Lake District. The seeming authenticity of the characters is greatly aided by the fact that Walpole used the surnames of people living in the valley at the time when the books were written.

Walpole loved Borrowdale, and although he was a much travelled man, he found tranquillity and peace in the valley that was unattainable elsewhere. Although he regarded Brackenburn as his home, he used it more as a retreat. He only stayed there for a few weeks at a time. Nevertheless, he became involved in many of the valley activities, and supported many causes. He was a generous man and donated to both the valley church and school. At the latter, there is still money that was given by Sir Hugh for a prize for the best composition written by a child at Borrowdale school. One former scholar recalls, " He gave all the children a pen for the Jubilee of George V, and a knife for the Coronation of George VI." When asked if the girls at the school were given knives, the reply came, "I don't know, I wasn't interested in girls then." Walpole, who never married, enjoyed nothing more than to sit high above the lake, totally absorbed by the changing moods of the landscape created by passing clouds, and light and shadow. When Walpole died in 1941 the seat was erected to his memory by his friend and secretary companion, Harold Cheevers.

To the Memory of Sir Hugh Walpole CBE
of Brackenburn
This seat is erected by his friend Harold Cheevers
Sept. 1941

Why not sit where Walpole spent many hours and recreate some of the feelings of awe, timelessness and space that he felt for the Lake District that inspired him to write;

Tales of a Lakeland Valley - BORROWDALE

"Over this country, when the giant Eagle flings the shadow of his wing, the land is darkened...From Whinlatter to Black Combe the clouds are never still. The Tarns like black unwinking eyes watch their chase, and the colours are laid out in patterns on the rocks and are continually changed. The Eagle can see the shadows rise from their knees at the base of Scafell and Gable, he can see the black precipitous flanks of the Screes washed with rain and the dark purple hummocks of Borrowdale crags flash suddenly with gold..."

Station 8. The final station that is to be found on this circular tour of Derwentwater, is set into the rock on the lower slopes of Catbells. This is one of the most popular fells among walkers in the Lake District, and very often it is the first to be climbed by visiting holiday makers. The memorial is to Thomas Arthur Leonard, who did a great deal to encourage people to take to the great outdoors in the years before it became an acceptable way to spend a holiday. He believed that many mill and factory workers who were tied to long, dark weary hours of work, could be physically, mentally and spiritually refreshed by enjoying the shared experience of open air life with like minded companions. Even though social conditions and circumstances have changed, the concept of communal holidays continues to flourish in Borrowdale with centres at Portinscale and Seatoller. The inscription on the tablet reads.

Thomas Arthur Leonard, Founder of the Co-operative and Communal Holidays and 'Father' of the Open - Air Movement in this country. Born London March 12 1864. Died Conway July 19 1948 Believing that 'The best things a mortal hath are those which every mortal shares.' He endeavoured to promote Joy in the widest communality spread.

Roadside memorial to William Hodgson

This was the original view of Grange from the roadside seat

Interior of Grange Church

CHAPTER THREE

Tales from the Old Days

There are few people who have lived in Grange as long as Alan Mounsey, for the hamlet has been his home for the best part of eighty years. His grandfather, who was descended from "The Kings of Patterdale", moved to Stonethwaite in 1857, and a few years later settled in Grange. Alan grew up in the village and attended the small one teacher school. "There was never many scholars there, and we only had the one teacher," he said. Miss Wedgewood was remembered as being "quite stern, and keen on theatricals."

Grange had more communal village life before the outbreak of the second world war than is the case today; and much of it revolved round both the church and chapel. "All the children used to go to Sunday School at the Methodist Chapel. It didn't matter whether they were chapel or Church of England. We were ecumenical in Grange before it was fashionable" said Dorothy Hind, who was also born in the village. She recalled that one high spot of the year was a magic lantern show that was held in the schoolroom; it showed the work of Anglican missionaries. "To us, it was like going to see Betty Grable," she commented, "it was something marvellous, we led very simple lives then." Whist drives, dances and Christmas parties in the big houses and hotels were all some of the activities that the community shared.

Links between Keswick, and the villages of the Borrowdale valley were, and still are, maintained by the Borrowdale bus service. Residents and old time visitors to the valley remember it with great affection, for the "Borro'dl bus" provided more than just transport; travel on the Borrowdale bus was a social experience!

Alan Mounsey's memory goes beyond the days of motorised transport, for he recalled that the first Borrowdale bus was old Willie Askew's horse bus on which he travelled as a lad. It carried about twelve passengers, who needed the aid of a ladder to clamber aboard, and it was pulled by two horses. Willie was an unflappable character, and Alan recalled the time a lady complained about the slowness of travel.

"Can't you go a little faster Mr Askew ?"

"What are you worrying about?" Willie replied, "You're having a longer ride."

Motor coaches began to make their appearance in the valley even while Willie Askew's horse bus was still plodding its way along the narrow road. One of the earliest belonged to Jack Pepper from Bowder Stone Cottage, and was known as the "Yellow Peril." The flattened surface of waste from the nearby quarries, that was built up into spoil heaps, provided an ideal site for the bus to be garaged in its wooden shed. In 1926, Addison Pepper built another garage for his bus in Grange, next to where the Methodist Chapel stands today. "In those days, Grange Cottage, which comes out to the road, was a stable and coach house, and Tommy Cockbain, one of the farm men there, used to butch sheep in the coach house. The horses of course were in the stable." Both of the Pepper buses were open topped vehicles which was ideal when the weather was fine, but on wet days, which was quite often, a canvas hood was pulled over from the back of the bus and side flaps were raised, which gave some degree of protection from the rain and wind.

This was the first motor bus in the valley that belonged to Mr Pepper. On this occasion it was used for the Mothers' Union trip in 1923

This restored "set pot" is now a feature of a farmhouse living room.

Tales of a Lakeland Valley - BORROWDALE

As more visitors began to visit the Lake District, the demand for public transport grew and the names of Simpson, Weightman, Youngs, Askew and Cumberland became familiar to those wanting to avoid a long tramp down the valley road. "After 1920, there were five different companies operating trips down the valley" said Alan. All five companies operated in the summer time but only two provided a winter service. "They didn't all run every day," recalled Willie Hind who lives at Stonethwaite. "It was an integrated service, they used to work it between them. It was a weird and wonderful timetable, but they got there."

The Borrowdale Bus also acted as a delivery service for valley folk. Willie Hind explained the system. " It was a way of shopping. You went to the public phone and rang up for what you wanted, and asked them to send it down on t' next bus. They just dropped it off at t' road end, and nobody ever touched it. Mind you, if it was a packet o' meat, and t' hunt was in, hound dogs might have a go at it."

The drivers became much loved characters, none more so than John Atkinson who used to drive for Simpsons. Willie recalled one of the stories about John Ackie's delivery service.

"There was a woman called Jinny Rigg that lived at Mountain View. John was going down in the bus one morning and she stopped him. Ah' ve gotta gaa til a weddin this efterneun, an' Ah evn't got a hat. Do you think you could just pop into John Henry Temple's on t' Main Street, an' git me a hat? Ye know the sort o' thing Ah weer.

Aye, alright, said John.

Tell him Ah'll pay him when Ah come in next time.

Anyway, John went away down to Keswick, landed with a hat and fetched it for her on t' next bus!"

Another of the bus drivers was Willie Young who was noted for packing so many passengers into his bus that there was hardly room for him to get into the driver's seat. "He would load them in at Seatoller, load them in at Mountain View and at Rosthwaite; he'd git to Grange and he'd be absolutely jam packed. There's plenty o' room at t' back, he'd shout. He daren't go into Keswick 'cos police 'd be at him for overloading. He used to stop at Castle Head and let a few out to walk into town.

Ah'll git arrested if Ah tek the lot o' you in, he would say."

It's said that some of the deep grooves in the surface of the Borrowdale road were caused by Willie Young's overloaded bus dragging its backside on the road.

At Grange today, there is a substantial stone shelter for the use of passengers while waiting for a bus, but this was not always the case. When the school in Grange closed down, it was only on condition that transport was provided to take the children to the "big" school at Rosthwaite. Grange parents refused to allow their children to travel on the bus until a shelter was built for them. The first was made of wood, which satisfied the parents sufficiently to allow their children to travel to school. Other valley children were not so fortunate, for they had a long walk from Seathwaite, Seatoller, and over the fell from Watendlath to reach school. Nowadays, private cars and school transport make school attendance an easy matter.

Willie Hind and his wife Dorothy both attended the old Victorian school that stood near to Stonethwaite road ends. "We did Swedish drill on the verandah, we had Scripture every day, reading, spelling, arithmetic and nature, and we recited our tables by rote. We seemed to pack such a lot into each day. Mr Scott was keen on woodwork and the older boys made a canoe that they sailed on the school field that always flooded in winter. We had concerts; some of the children were quite musical and played solos or accompaniments. Mr Scott did his best to teach us to play the violin. Can you imagine what it sounded like?"

When Alan Mounsey left school, he began work with the family's long established joinery business at Grange, and he recalled his early working days as a joiner. "We had a certain amount of standing timber that we felled and left to season," Alan explained. When the wood had to be cut into manageable lengths, there was no easy flick of a switch to stir an electric saw in to life. "We had an old oil engine which was heated up with a blow lamp. You'd to get that red hot and then pull this huge fly wheel back on to compression, and plop, she would go, but only if she was in the mood! Sometimes if you got flooded with oil, you had a bit of trouble."

Once the engine was working it provided the necessary power to drive the saw. The timber was brought as close to the workshop as possible, from where it was hauled inside by a cumbersome, but effective device. "It was a long chain with a hook on; and that had a roller, like a mangle roller, which the chain went round, and it was fastened onto a pulley round a beam, and that was geared to a handle. It originally belonged to Tom Pape who was a butcher in Keswick, and it was used for dragging cows and carcasses and then my grandfather bought it off him when he packed in."

Alan explained that his family business used to make the hammers and mallets for the quarrymen of Honister. "We got our shafts out of ash grown on our own land, and matured it until it was seasoned. They had to be cut to the correct thicknesses with the saw. My grandfather first, and then my uncle would go to Liverpool for the African oak that we used for the hammer or mallet heads. Our own oak wasn't hard enough. Callipers were used to make sure that everything was made to the correct fraction of an inch. They had to have a little bit of taper to the shaft . They were sent up to the quarry where they had their own blacksmith and he would put the iron hoops on the head." Mallets were also sent to the quarries at Balachulish in Scotland, as well as to some of the slate workings of North Wales. "I used to tek them to Keswick station packed in wooden cases that tinned fruit came in. All I had to put on the label was Balachulish Slate Quarries, via Oban, and they got there."

Another of the jobs that the Mounsey's carried out was the repair of rowing boats. "Nearly all the boarding houses round about had a boat which they kept on the lake. You see, folks couldn't just ride around like they do now. Boating on Derwentwater, and down the river, and fishing was the thing to do. We used to repair boats with larch planks, and we used to store two in the loft, up on the cross beams of the main principals. They were done up, painted and varnished each spring, and they were put in the river to start with to swell, because they'd been dry all winter. And then we took them down to the lake where we had our special anchorage."

The Mounsey family had a close association with quarrying, for the Quay Foot quarries were once owned by a Joseph Robinson, a relative of both Alan, and Kenneth Robinson of Troutdale. " I suppose they stopped working during the first world war; then

Honister Quarries took them over and now they belong to the National Trust. There was a gap at the top end of the spoil heap where the rail lines for wheeling the bogeys of slate across the road passed through. The dressing and riving sheds were also on top of that spoil heap, and that left the quarry area free for blasting."

These quarries were once known locally as The Fairy Caves, and were described as being "ancient workings" in Henry Jenkinson's Guide book to the Lake District. They are marked on the current Ordnance Survey map as Quay Foot quarries, but local people refer to them as Whye Foot quarries. A possible explanation for the difference in names may be found in A. C. Gibson's book, "Folk Speech, Tales and Rhymes of Cumberland, 1868. *"Why"* is a dialect word for a heifer, and *"quie"*, and *"quiga"* have the same meanings in Old Norse and Danish respectively. At one time, the spoil heaps from those quarries used to tumble down to the road, but in the 1950's, the National Trust made the decision to grass them over, and a casual visitor to the valley would find it hard to believe that the grassy mounds were once the debris of a thriving industry.

Close by the quarries, and situated on the rough road that was once a well used route through the valley, can be found the Bowder Stone. This is a single rock of tremendous dimensions. It is estimated to be about 2,000 tons in weight and it stands over 30 feet in height. It was probably deposited in Borrowdale as a result of glaciation movement. It has been a popular attraction for visitors since they first started exploring the valley in the 18th century. *"In the middle of one of the recesses of the valley lies an enormous stone; which is called in the country Boother Stone. Massy rocks of immense size rent from mountains, are everywhere to be found: but this stone appears to be of a different kind. It does not seem to have been the appendage of a mountain; but itself an independent creation. It lies in a sort of diagonal position; overshadowing a space, sufficient to shelter a troop of horse."* wrote William Gilpin in 1772.

Visitors to the Bowder Stone leave the horse drawn carriage to enjoy the view.

Tales of a Lakeland Valley - BORROWDALE

Until the latter years of the 1930's, it was possible for visitors to order an afternoon tea, or buy postcards from Bowder Stone Cottage. Kenneth Robinson, recalled that, "You really got a good tea there. If we had visitors and didn't know what to do with them, we took them to Bowder Stone for Mrs Pepper's afternoon tea."

A number of little shelters made of rustic poles gave a degree of privacy to those who wanted to "take tea" in an idyllic setting. Plates full of home baked bread, cakes and scones, with home made jam from fruit grown in the garden or gathered from the hedgerows; lashings of cream and strawberries when they were in season, were enjoyed by visitor and locals alike. At one time, a visitors' book was kept at the Bowder Stone for those to sign who were adventurous enough to climb the ladder to reach the top of the stone.

Many of the more modern houses in and around Grange were built by the Mounseys, and it was through this work that Alan met Sir Hugh Walpole, the eminent writer. "You felt there was a bit of something special about him. He was a tall good looking chap. Uncle George met him at Keswick station to take him to see Brackenburn. The family did a lot of work for him over the years. We raised Brackenburn to two stories for him." Hugh Walpole became very friendly with George Mounsey, and was a frequent visitor to Grange. He used the Mounsey surname for characters in the books of his Herries Chronicles, as he did with many other of the valley folk.

The Keswick building firm of Abbots worked alongside the Mounseys on the enlarging of Brackenburn. "It was a red hot day in August, and John Snowdon, who was working on the roof was stripped off to the waist. The sky was full of flying ants in columns, all swirling round with gulls darting in among them. Suddenly all the ants came down in a cloud and completely covered John. They didn't bother the rest of us."

Alan built a house in Grange which Sir Hugh Walpole bought, and named it "Copperfield". It is situated opposite the church and the name is unusual in an area that displays such names as "High Rigg" engraved on slate signs. Alan explained how it came about. "Sir Hugh bought it as a home for his gardener and handyman. It was also big enough to provide accommodation for any important people that came to visit him. J.B Priestly often came, as well as other writers. He liked to be on his own, he didn't like visitors getting under his feet. He paid £910 for the house, and said that he paid for it with money he had earned writing the scenario for the film production of "David Copperfield" in America. So he called the house after the film. He spent quite a lot of time at Brackenburn. He was the sort of fella who lived it up a bit in London, and then he came up here to recuperate. He would stay for about six weeks at a time. He had diabetes, and died after going into a coma. Pneumonia set in and old Dr Cameron couldn't pull him round."

Death was no stranger to Alan Mounsey, for as a joiner, he made coffins for many of those who died in the valley. He recalled one tragedy with which he was involved that happened during the winter of 1940.

"Joe Pepper had gone to the lake with his dog. The dog ran on to the ice and fell in the water at a duck hole. Joe ran to the Lodore boat house and got a plank which he laid on the ice." At the edge of the lake where the ice was thick, it was strong enough to support the crawling weight of Joe and the plank. As he approached the duck hole, the ice became thinner, and more fragile. The combination of a slight movement from roosting ducks and a greater depth of water, was sufficient to prevent the continuation of a thick ice layer. As Joe approached the hole, the plank broke through the ice and Joe slid under the surface. Alan was one of those who went to look for him.

"It was frozen very thick, and we went down to look for him. We found his rifle on the gravel. We followed two sets of footsteps down to the duck hole, but only one set coming back. And so we gave it up , do y' see. It told its own tale. The dog got out and landed back home covered in icicles. That was January 18th 1940. It was that terrible deep snow then. There wasn't much when we went to look for him, there was just a flurry, then it came on really heavy. One weekend it put eighteen inches of snow down. Well by the next week, that eighteen had gone to nine; see, it went solid, and then it came another eighteen on top of it."

The snow was so deep that the hearse for the funeral had to be dug out of the snow. "It was an east wind, and at Stonethwaite, it blows right through. As fast as snow was cleared, it filled in again. From Rosthwaite to Stonethwaite they had the Dickens of a job to get it out. At Stonethwaite, it was a different kettle o' fish to Grange, we are sheltered here, but there they had level snow."

Willie Hind who has spent most of his life in Stonethwaite, remembers it very well. "That 1940 job, that really was a bad winter. It snowed us in here completely. When I got up in the morning, the snow was up to the top of the windows. It was just a white wall, and when you opened the door, you couldn't see out! Fortunately we had the fire shovel and we dug a way out." Getting away out of the house was not the end of the story for Willie, for like so many cottages in the valley, they were still dependent on paraffin lamps. "I walked to Keswick from here to get paraffin, that was what we needed for the lamps and the Primus stove to boil the kettle. The rest of the cooking was done on the fire. There was a little side boiler , where you got hot water, and then there was a big range with a trivet on the front where you put pans and things, at the other side there was an oven."

Willie walked to Keswick carrying a two gallon can to be filled with paraffin. "It was easier walking through the fields. There was four or five foot of snow on the roads, but hardly any on the fields. You just climbed dykes and wa's as you came at them." Willie managed to get back on the Borrowdale Bus with John Ackie, who was able to reach Borrowdale Hotel, "but he couldn't get any further."

Parts of the cottage in which Willie and his wife live date back to the 17th century, but over the years, the little complex of buildings have been altered, added to, and enlarged The old wash house is still there. "All the washing was done there there was a set pot in the corner with a grate underneath and you used to fire it with long lumps of wood or any old stuff, and boil her up and away she would go. The tubs were emptied down the drain; the drains went underground and eventually found the way to the river. All the old drainage is still there; it still operates."

Willie recalled that there used to be three farms in Stonethwaite, but it was basically subsistence farming that went on. "The man worked elsewhere, probably at Honister Quarries and he did his farming in the evenings and at weekends. Everybody mucked in to give a hand, even those that didn't live on the farms. We yoked horses, and lead carts to where they were needed even though we had nowt to do with the farm. Every farm had a bit of arable land to grow their vegetables, and they had a few cows for milk that they sold round t' village."

"Everybody was very equal in those days. You either had, or you hadn't; and there was more of those that hadn't," commented Dorothy.

In the days following the end of the second world war, ex- serviceman Owen Dennison was a familiar figure on the road that led from Grange to Manesty. Gates used to straddle the road that rises across the lower slopes of Catbells, and which overlooks Derwentwater. Owen used to "guard" the Manesty gate. "He was one of the last of the gatemen. He was an ex serviceman from the second world war. He opened the gate as a way of making a few bob. He use to sell bottles of pop to cyclists and walkers from his little wooden hut. I've had many a one. He limped quite badly, and dragged a foot; it was always exaggerated a bit when he went to open the gate. He used to come down the valley on the Borrowdale bus every morning and back again to Keswick at night with his little terrier dog. If it had been a warm day he went back at night with a face the colour of the rising sun," said Kenneth Robinson as he recalled his memories of Owen Dennison.

Although Owen's "sentry box" and the gate have long since gone, the gate stoups still remain at a narrow part of the road that is only wide enough to allow one car to pass through. Recommendations have been made that the stoups should be removed in the interests of widening the road, but they are still there, to remind of a slower, and less frenetic way of life!

Stonethwaite, the end of the road for motor vehicles.

CHAPTER FOUR

Murder in the Valley

When Judge Humphreys wrote his book about some of the murders with which he was involved, he described "The Chinese Murder" as the first murder to take place in Cumberland for over forty years. It occurred in Borrowdale on 19 June 1928, when Wai Sheung Sui Miao aged 29 was killed, and her husband, 28 year old Dr Chung Yi Miao was accused of her murder. Wai Sheung was the daughter of a wealthy Cantonese mandarin, she was highly educated and travelled extensively. She met Chung at a New York party in October of 1927, and they became infatuated with each other. Although Chung had only recently completed his law studies, he came from a family with good connections that were acceptable to Wai Sheung's family. They married in New York on 12 May 1928, and sailed across the Atlantic to spend their honeymoon in Scotland and England. They travelled by train to Keswick from Edinburgh, and arrived by taxi at the Borrowdale Gates Hotel, on June 18.

When the murder occurred, "I was on the spot, so to speak," said Alan Mounsey. "In those days, we had quite a lot of logs and timber to drag in to saw. We used to congregate there at night, a lot of us, after the evening meal for a chat. Well there was nothing much else to do. There was no television, well there was radio, a certain amount, but not many folks had them. We were all standing or sitting around on the wood, and the old gentleman Tom Wilson from Castle Crag came up and told us what he had seen. Old Tom had more or less given up farming, and every day he used to tek his little dog for a walk along by the river then up on the fell."

Alan explained that there were three routes up from the river through Cummacatta Wood that the local people used to follow, on what was a regular walk for many of them. That night, at about 7.30 pm. Tom had used the central route which Alan described as, "rather easier." Tom followed the path, and when he got towards the top he saw something strange. "He said I saw what looked like a woman lying with her head down hill, and her parasol up, and her legs up in the air." He told the listening group of Grange men that he didn't want to disturb her, and so came back a different way.

"He didn't really know what he had seen" said Alan, "but as people kept joining our group, old Tom would repeat the tale again, and it began to bother him. Walter Birkett, who was the postmaster at the time, came with his little white Sealyham dog and Tom told him. One of Pepper's came, and he told him, then Walter's wife Martha came, and old Tom repeated the story. He was really bothered. I came across this body with her head downhill and her parasol up, and her feet up in t' air. And he kept saying this to everybody that came. ·

Martha Birkett said, There's something queer about this. I think some of you chaps had better go and see. If none of you's keen to go, I'll go myself. So me dad and Joe Pepper agreed to go and have a look."

They crossed Grange Bridge, and turned right down the valley road to where a wicket gate allowed access to Cummacatta Wood. "Dad went on his bike and got there before

Joe and sure enough she was black in t' face; she'd been strangled. He could see she was dead as soon as he got there. He was just looking at her when Joe came up from the river bank. Dad shouted down, She's dead. Joe turned on his heels and he was back at that group on the logs before me dad got there on his bike."

The two village men were accompanied by Detective Pendlebury, who was on holiday at Grange. He was related to George Mounsey, and was able to report with professional clarity what they found. The sight that had caused Tom Wilson such agitation was the body of a woman with three strangulation cords round her neck; her clothes were in disarray and there was blood trickling from her ears, nose, and mouth. The woman was Chinese, and matched the description of one that Pendlebury had seen earlier that day, arm in arm with a tall Chinaman.

"Pendlebury had eyes that always used to be flashing from one side to another, and he took it all in, well that was his business, his trade as a policeman and he was able to give evidence that he recognised them as the Chinese couple that were staying at the Borrowdale Gates Hotel." As soon as he returned to Grange, Detective Constable Pendlebury phoned the Keswick police to notify them of the gruesome discovery. This was at about 8.50 p.m., and Inspector Graham came to Borrowdale immediately to confront the Chinaman, who had been seen returning alone to the hotel at about four o clock.

The body was left on the fell and George Mounsey was asked to go and stay with it. "He said they didn't come back, and it was getting dark. He saw a figure coming across the field, it was a hay field then, it's just a swamp now. He said, it was coming right towards 'm. I wonder if this is whoever done the murder come to have a look at t' body, he said. It turned out to be Mrs Jenkinson havin' a walk out from Hollows Farm." Eventually, and as a result of the phone call to Keswick police, Dr Robert Crawford , a local GP was sent to examine the body.

His report indicated that he found the woman lying on her back in between two large boulders, with the legs drawn up and the feet together. Although rigor mortis had set in, Dr. Crawford estimated that death had occurred between 2.30 p.m. and 5 p.m.. There were three cords round her neck; one was a green window cord, tied in a reef knot on the right hand side. It was four feet five inches long. The second cord, which was wrapped round the neck three times, was five feet two inches long and was also fastened in a reef knot on the same side as the other. Underneath these two cords was a doubly twisted string that was embedded into the victim's neck and fastened with a granny knot on the right hand side. In the doctor's opinion, this had been the cause of death, which he was sure had been instantaneous. The blood coming from the woman's ear, nose and mouth suggested violence, but there was no sign that a struggle had taken place. The discovery of blood in a fissure of some other rocks, suggested the body had been moved. There was a glove on the right hand of the body, but the glove of the left hand had been peeled off, and the ring finger of the left hand showed marks where rings had once been worn. An open umbrella shielded her face.

At the Borrowdale Gates Hotel, Inspector Graham knocked on the door of Room Number 5. "They had the same room, that my aunty Polly jumped from the window when she went to school there," said Alan Mounsey.

Chung was in bed, to which he had retired at 10pm after eating his evening meal alone. He complained of having a bad cold and explained that his wife had gone to buy some warmer clothes in Keswick that afternoon. He expressed some concern to the hotel proprietor, Miss Crossley at the none appearance of his wife, and she offered to phone

Keswick to see if any explanation could be found. Other guests were also concerned as they had found the Chinese couple very happy in each other's company

Inspector Graham told Chung to get dressed immediately. He informed him that his wife's body had been found, and he was being detained on suspicion of causing death by strangling. Room Number 5 was searched, and although Chung denied any knowledge of the whereabouts of the keys to his wife's jewellery case, a set of seven keys was found in Chung's bag. One of the key's fitted the case. The police also found a shirt in Chung's bag, and wrapped in its folds was a valuable pearl necklace that Wai Sheung had been wearing earlier that day.

Chung was arrested and taken to Keswick Police Station. Inspector Graham commented of Chung that, "he appeared to show some emotion." Although the Chinaman was not as fluent in English as his wife had been, he did understand what was happening and protested his innocence. "It is terrible my wife assaulted, robbed and murdered. Find who has her jewellery and you will have the killer."

During a further search of Chung's room, two unprocessed rolls of Kodak films were found, these were handed over to Henry Mayson, the well known Keswick photographer. He opened the small packages; one contained a roll of unexposed film; but when he opened the foil and waxed paper wrapping of the other, two rings tumbled out. One was a diamond solitaire, the other a slim platinum band set with diamonds on which was inscribed "C.Y.M. 12.5.28", the date of their marriage. Wai Sheung had been seen wearing these rings on the day of the murder. The remaining jewellery in the locked case, was valued at almost three and a half thousand pounds.

Chung was held in custody while enquiries and further investigations were made. When he was finally brought before the court on 31 July, a large crowd had gathered, among them was Hugh Walpole. Competition for places was intense, but there was only room for a few in the small court room. Chung's clothes had been taken to be examined for blood stains, and he emerged from the car that brought him to court wrapped in a grey blanket. He appeared smiling and cheerful when he was put into the dock, and nodded to his lawyers and interpreter. He admitted there were blood stains on the fawn overcoat that he had worn on the day of the murder, but explained those had been acquired in New York. He denied killing his wife, and insisted that she had gone to Keswick to buy some warm clothes. He explained that Wai Sheung told him to go back to his room to rest in a warm bed, to see if he could ease his cold.

The evidence against him seemed overwhelming. He had been seen returning to Grange by DC Pendlebury at about 4 p.m., who described the Chinaman as "hurrying and looking extremely pale." Cords, similar to those used in the strangulation, were found in a cupboard in Room Number 5, although none of the remaining cord was of the same colour. The hotel staff reported that on his return, the Chinaman had appeared distraught, and had been heard pacing up and down his room. Then there was the discovery of the jewellery hidden away, and investigation into his affairs revealed he was of very limited financial means.

It was accepted that all the evidence against him was circumstantial, and Chung continued to protest his innocence. He claimed that he and his wife had been followed from Edinburgh by another Chinese couple, who had been seen in the area around Grange quite recently. However, all the sightings of Chinese people in the valley that were given by a large number of independent witnesses fitted the descriptions of Chung and his wife. There was opportunity for murder; there was motive for murder, but had he actually killed his wife?

Tales of a Lakeland Valley - BORROWDALE

After six long weeks of court appearances and investigation at Keswick, Chung was sent for trial to Carlisle Assizes where Judge Humphreys heard the case on 22 November 1928. The trial lasted for three days, but it only took the jury an hour to deliver a verdict of Guilty. Judge Humphreys passed sentence of death.

Chung appealed and the case was taken to London where it was heard at the Court of Criminal Appeal on November 19. Chung conducted his own defence. He produced three witnesses who confirmed Chung's own statement that there were two other orientals in the area. John Abraham, the Grange postmaster said he had seen them at Keswick railway station on the morning of the 20 June getting on the Penrith train, but they were not carrying any luggage. In spite of Chung's own attempt to clear his name, and a petition for clemency from Carlisle which contain 800 names, there was no reversal of the death sentence. Chung was taken to Strangeways Prison, in Manchester.

There he was hanged on December 6 1928.

That was not the complete end to the story. Chung's mother came to England and brought with her a letter she had received from her son that contained startling information. It provided evidence that Chung was a bigamist. He told his mother not only of his "marriage" to Wai Sheung, but that he had also received a letter sent from his legal wife in China, informing him that she was coming to England to visit him. In the letter, Chung told his mother that he loved his legal wife more than Wai Sheung, and must end the affair. Chung is reputed to have received the letter from his legal wife about the time that he and Wai Sheung arrived in Borrowdale!

In January of 1929, the body of Wai Sheung was exhumed from her simple grave at Crosthwaite and taken back to China in a double coffin of lead and ornamental gold. Once in her home country, she was given three ceremonial funerals, the last of which was held in Canton and attended by a hundred professional mourners, twelve bands and followed by a procession a mile long.

The case was reported in great detail in the local papers, where the "West Cumberland Times" carried graphic accounts of each day's proceedings. As the details of the case were discussed around the big kitchen table in Alan Mounsey's home, his twelve year old ears picked up information about new evidence that came to light. "I was that scared, my mother had to move into my room, and I slept with my dad." he said.

The passing of time has erased much of the memory of that gruesome murder in such a peaceful place, although it developed an eerie and frightening association for the youngsters who grew up in the valley. "Of course, you got ghost stories about it", Kenneth Robinson recalled. "If you were up that end of the valley and it was dark, the old bike came fast round those corners."

CHAPTER FIVE

Any Old Iron

A track crosses the beck at Rosthwaite to lead either over the fell to Watendlath, or a right turn takes one alongside the river to the hamlet of Stonethwaite. Motorists may prefer to drive a short distance south to Stonethwaite road ends before turning left to reach the hamlet. From that point, the valleys of Greenup and Langstrath can only be explored on foot or by cycle.

The becks that flow through these valleys meet at a junction marked on the Ordnance Survey map as Smithymire Island. Anyone with an inquiring turn of mind must wonder at the significance of the name, for its association with the forging of iron is too tempting to ignore. A further clue can be gained from the map where the name of Ore Gap is to be found below Bow Fell. This is the mountain that heads the Langstrath valley, and with a little more detective groundwork, and the recession of one's imagination back in time to almost five hundred years, one of the Lake District's earliest industries can be explored.

The eminent historian, W.G Collingwood, refers in his book "History of Cumberland", to a bloomery in the Langstrath Valley. A bloomery is an old iron smelting site, and Collingwood dates the Langstrath site as going back to medieval times. It is thought that nearly all bloomery sites are to to be found close to running water. The flattened area of ground, with its few birch trees is initially an insignificant looking area, but a close examination can reveal hard, dark fragments of metal embedded in the earth.

There is a strange sensation of wonder to ease a piece out of the ground and hold the red brown iron that has lain there, untouched for so many years. Sufficient pieces of slag and iron were easily visible over an extensive area, to become aware that this was indeed an iron making site of some antiquity and importance. There was further evidence to be found in a grassy bank nearby which showed a blackened edge. Many walkers must have passed this by without realising there was any significance to this blackness, but a gentle probing revealed that it was not a bank of earth, but a bank of charcoal. Embedded in the blackened and aged embers were more pieces of iron; here was a further tangible link with years gone by.

The rain poured down on that February day of my first exploratory visit to the site. There was a rushing roar from the two becks as they surged down their respective valleys, meeting in a turbulence of foaming, icy green water . The wind howled down the valley of Langstrath, yet in my mind, I was back with the iron makers of long ago. A small piece of iron was my transport for that mental journey. Its upper surface was smooth, yet slightly pitted, along one edge was a rippling fold of metal reminiscent of a lava flow. In colour, it was reddish brown intermingled with darker shades of brown or black. The underside was roughly wrinkled where bubbles of molten metal had exploded and then solidified. Colours of orange and yellow showed through while in the creases of the metal, tiny seeds were locked away.

How long had the metal been lying there? Who were those early smiths? How had the iron been made? These were questions which needed to be answered to create a picture of the Cumbrians who lived and worked in the valley hundreds of years ago.

Man discovered how to use iron thousands of years ago, but iron making in the Borrowdale valley of Langstrath was closely associated with the two great Cistercian abbeys of Furness and Fountains. The influence of the monasteries as powerful landowners developed in the years following the Norman Conquest. The erection of monastic buildings throughout England was on a par with the defensive system of castles that were erected by the conquering Norman knights, and there seemed little to choose between the administration of their land, and the dues that were exacted from their tenants. Many of the early abbots were not noted for their holiness, or gentle ways. They were powerful rulers of their domains.

Furness Abbey and Fountains Abbey between them owned most of the land in Borrowdale, but the area around Stonethwaite was always in dispute, for this held some of the richest farming land in the valley; it was ideal for dairy farming. The disputed ownership was not resolved until 1303, when the Crown reclaimed the land, and sold it to Fountains Abbey for a sum of forty shillings. The divide was made, Fountains owned the land extending into Greenup from Stonethwaite, while Furness held Langstrath.

Iron making had been an important part of Furness Abbey's economy, for it is recorded that in 1269, one sixth of the Abbey's profits was obtained from iron making in the Furness area. The abbey was situated in an area where it was able to exploit the deposits of rich hematite ore of Furness, and employ local people to cut timber and convert it into charcoal for smelting. All the necessary requirements for making iron were to be found in the Langstrath valley, and the expertise of the monastic landlord was able to direct, and develop the industry.

It is almost certain that the raw iron ore was brought by pack animal from the rich deposits that are found above Angle Tarn, where even today the ground is heavily stained red from the underlying ore. Ore Gap, which is between Bowfell and Esk Pike was referred to as Orscarth in 1242, and may be derived from the name, "Orsgarth," the collecting place of the ore.

The steep fell sides of the Langstrath valley are bare today, with hardly a tree in sight, but imagine if you can, that same valley densely covered with trees. Oak, rowan , holly and birch completely covered the fell sides. The route that Langstrath beck had carved for itself through the hard volcanic rock afforded the only easy passage through the valley. The Furness monks set their tenants to work to fell and clear areas of woodland to turn raw timber into charcoal. This was an ideal slow burning, but intensely hot fuel to convert the raw iron ore into a malleable metal in simple furnaces. It has been calculated that six loads of wood were needed to make one load of charcoal, and it was deemed more economic of time and labour to bring the ore to the charcoal making sites. Water was also needed, not only for the personal use of the workers, but to damp down the smouldering fuel so that it would not burn too rapidly.

Tales of a Lakeland Valley - BORROWDALE

Although there was such a wealth of timber, the valley folk were not allowed to fell trees for their own use. The trees belonged to the Abbot, and were to be used as he directed, the only concession made was that valley dwellers could gather dead or blown wood that had come down in storms. This was sometimes sold by the gatherers for charcoal making and provided a useful supplement to the meagre income that they made. While no direct reference of payment in Borrowdale has been found, there is a record of thirty shillings being paid *"for the sale of dead wood to the bloomeries at Buttermere and Hobcarton"* which dates from 1290. It is more than likely that a similar practise was followed in Borrowdale.

Iron making in a bloomery is said to have been a simple process. *"If a lump of red or brown hematite be heated for a few hours in a charcoal furnace, well bedded with fuel, it will be more or less easily reduced so as to admit of being easily forged, at a red heat, into a bar of iron."*

The furnace or hearth , the name by which it was often referred, could have been a hole in the ground, or a hole let into a bank side. When it was the former, it often took the shape of an inverted hat, with the crown inserted into the ground, and the broad brim shallowing to the surface. Sometimes it was nothing more than a "cylinder of clay held together with hoops of cane." If the hole in the ground method was used, the hollow was given a charcoal lining, that was then set alight. This was covered with crushed or broken ore, and then given a further covering of charcoal. The admission of air through vents was essential to raise the temperature of the furnace and to control the intensity of the heat. Furnaces that were built into the Langstrath fellside incorporated vents that made use of the valley winds. At lower, or sheltered levels. air was mechanically driven into the furnace by the operation of a primitive pump. "...bellows made of goat skin, or a hollow stem of a tree packed with feathers or other material." Hand or foot power was required to operate this simple forge.

The fact that iron was so highly prized in the 14th century is indicated by the fact that there were frequent raids by marauding Borderers who penetrated into the Borrowdale valley, or even ventured as far south as Furness. During the period of the Dissolution of the Monasteries, nearly all land under the control of the great abbeys or monasteries was confiscated by the Crown, and subsequently re -let, or leased for the revenue that it raised, and a degree of control was exercised over the making of iron. In 1564, iron making in most of the Borrowdale bloomeries was forbidden by Royal decree. All available charcoal that was manufactured in the valley was needed to smelt the more valuable ores of copper, lead and silver that were being mined in Borrowdale and Newlands under the "Mines Royal" development. As a result of this decree, the main Borrowdale bloomeries declined into *"utter Ruyane and decaye."*

Some small bloomeries were allowed to continue on a none profit making basis to allow for the needs of local people. But all charcoal had to be made from fallen or storm blown wood; no wood cutting for the purpose of charcoal making was allowed.

As the mining of copper, lead and silver became more difficult and expensive, the activities of the Mines Royal declined early in the 17th century and the demand for charcoal in the industry was subsequently reduced. Bloomeries were allowed to develop again, and with increased technology brought into England by European workers, water powered wheels were introduced to drive the bellows to blow the still primitive furnaces. The last reference to a bloomery in Cumbria is in 1666, the year of the Great Fire of London. In that year, a licence was granted to the Manor of Hawkshead to fell trees and use water power to maintain a smithy. The rent was fixed at £20 a year, to be paid on the feast day of St. Michael the Archangel.

The large scale felling of trees for charcoal making caused the valleys to become deforested and the natural regeneration of timber was not rapid enough to keep up with the demand for wood. The cost of making charcoal became prohibitively high, and by 1727, half the cost of producing iron was for the charcoal alone. Fifty years later, this had risen to three quarters of the cost of iron production. Eventually, the development of coal mining transformed the iron making process when it became a major industry in West Cumbria.

Looking at the former bloomery sites in the Langstrath valley today, it is difficult to imagine the scene as it was hundreds of years ago, when the red ore was trundled from the high places, through forested fell sides to a smelting site beside a beck. Yet the links are there. The same beck still tumbles in its narrow gorge beside the bloomery site, fragments of iron lie embedded in the ground and a charcoal bank helps to supply tangible evidence of an ancient industry. Its age is indecisive for although Collingwood dates it to 1500, other sources such as Bernard Smith in his book, "Iron Ores", puts it at over 100 years later. Possibly only a carbon fibre dating of the charcoal would give a definitive answer for the scientifically inclined, while for the more romantic, there is the image of men and women toiling in the windswept valley when the first Elizabeth was queen.

Smithymire Island

Sarah Youdale's grave in Borrowdale Churchyard, is in the left foreground.

Interior of Borrowdale Church. The pulpit was brought from Mardale when that church was demolished prior to the flooding of the valley

CHAPTER SIX

Sarah Youdale - Queen of Borrowdale

The isolated nature of many of the Lake District valleys meant that the head of the family which assumed greatest importance, became the self styled king. The Holmes of Mardale, and the Mounseys of Patterdale are quite well documented as to their "kingdoms." Not so well known is King John Youdale of Borrowdale. When he died, his niece Sarah Youdale assumed the title of Queen when, as far as she was aware, she was the only surviving member of the family. In 1868 when talking of the decline of the long established Borrowdale families, she said, "Ah's still here, but Ah's last of us, widoot oor Hugh or Gawin left some bairns an' if they did it's mickle if they ivver come to Borro'dle."

Sarah Youdale was born in 1768, at a time when Borrowdale was a remote valley, cut off from the outside world. The tenants of distant landlords and the statesmen farmers were left very much to manage their own affairs. It was virtually a self contained community until the mid part of the 19th century, when tourists began to make their appearance to follow the journeys of such early explorers as Thomas Gray, the poet and clergyman William Gilpin.

Sarah was born shortly before Thomas Gray made his journey into the valley in 1769. Gray was reluctant to proceed much beyond Lodore because of the fearful tumbling of rocks from the fell sides that blocked his way. An unhappy and frightening experience in the Coniston area had made him wary of the uncertain stability of the crags. There was no road into the Borrowdale valley as we know it today. The main route was actually that used by pack horses that crossed the fell to Watendlath. That hamlet was at the crossroads of routes to Armboth, Keswick and Rosthwaite. The only other access that roughly followed the course of the river, was by means of a narrow track that wound in and out of the rocks; on its way by passing the Bowder Stone. It was only wide enough for pedestrians or horses. No one outside the valley would have taken much interest, or even been aware of the newly born baby who was to live to the ripe old age of 100, and die in February 1869 in her 101st year. A remarkable achievement in those days of infant mortality and generally short lives.

Sarah's education was very much related to working round the house and on the farm. She learned to bake, to sew, to spin wool, and generally manage a house. She learned which wild berries and herbs could be eaten or used for medicinal purposes and cures. She poulticed and patched inflammation on men and beasts. She worked in the fields from dawn till dusk making maximum use of the daylight hours. She gathered wood, and stacked the peats brought down from the mosses high on the fell.

If formal education was denied the Borrowdale lasses, then the lads had the opportunity to be taught by by the local priest, which in Sarah's opinion, resulted in a far higher standard of achievement than that being attained by the valley children in the 1860's. "Theer were better scholars lang sen than there are noo, twenty times ower.

T'skeul was nearly allus towt by t' priest, an' ivvery farmer's son was kept gaan to t' skeul t'l he was varra nar twenty. ... It isn't master's fault they're sek poor scholars noo, for barns nobbut 'tent laal bits, an' then they're tekin' off an' kept idlin' aboot yam; larnin' nowt at a'."

Sarah recalled that when she was a young lass, wheeled traffic had not entered the valley. It was very much an isolated and self sufficient community for the Crosthwaite Parish records show that in 1793, when Sarah was 24, there were 361 people living in the valley and these were outnumbered by sheep of which there were about 9,000.

What has changed? we may ask.

"When Ah was young there wasn't as mickle as a wheel thing in Borro'dl; nut that it mattered much for there were nee roads then, nobbut nags and foot folk."

In their every day work in the valley, Sarah and her companions never found the need for carts, for as she said, there was nowhere the carts could have gone. The work of ploughing, sowing, reaping and threshing was done by hand, or with the help of simple horse drawn machinery. Oats was one of their basic commodities for this provided the coarse oatmeal which formed their staple food, especially when made into haver bread which lasted for weeks when kept in the wooden oak chests. Each family kept a cow or two to provide milk and the occasional luxury of butter or cheese; while the occasional butching of a pig offered a variation from the ever present mutton that was wandering around on the hoof.

A description of the agricultural way of life is given in Hutchinson's History of Cumberland which was compiled over the years 1794 to 1797, when Sarah was in her mid to late twenties.

"They plough twice for wheat... They also stir twice for barley...For oats they stir but once. They have no beans, very few peas, and as little rye... They stir three times for turnips, hoe them once or twice...use them for feeding sheep and stall fatting oxen... They have two ways of cultivating potatoes, by ploughing and digging: in the first they stir three times and dung their land well, lay the slices in every other furrow, one foot asunder, and plough between them once, while growing, besides hand weeding. Their other way is the lazy bed method: they lay the dung on the green sward, the slices on that, when they dig the trenches, and with the earth cover the sets, but they reckon ploughing a better way."

Yields from this sort of farming ranged from twenty times the amount sown for wheat and barley, to a seven times return for oats. They harvested between two and four hundred bushels of potatoes for an acre which made it another of their staple food items.

Sheep were essential to the survival of Sarah and the rest of the valley folk. Four sheep could graze easily on an acre of grassland, although they required much more on the coarser grasses of the fells. The average selling price of a sheep was 4/3d.

The sheep provided not only the meat that was used in the boilings of the set pot, when even a sheep's head provided a tasty broth, but their wool from the fleeces was turned into cloth from which their clothes were roughly fashioned. Every summer there was the excitement of the gather, when each family would be helped by their neighbours to bring the sheep to the clipping sheds. Menfolk would move from farm to farm taking their own clipping stool and shears, cottagers would bring their few sheep to the clippin' and enjoy the opportunity to change a working day into a social occasion. Other folk would spend time on the fell to gather half cast fleeces or torn wool that sheep had left behind as they struggled in bracken or thorn. Each family was responsible for making their own clothes which they did from the cloth that was woven from the wool off the sheep's backs. "Ivverybody lived on their own produce, and were clad wid yam mead cloth. There wasn't a farm house but ye med hard through a' t' lang winter neets, whirring and burring o' t' wheels." Everybody in the family helped with some of the tasks, and as the wheels turned and the yarn was spun, tales of boggles and superstitions were told in the darkened rooms. The only light came from a fire's glow, or in some cases was provided by rush tapers that had been dipped in mutton fat over and over again to be made into candles. "Aye there were boggles plenty, but a' Ah ivver saw was nowt warse n' mysel'. But my uncle, King John, was yance terribly freeten'd. He was choppin' bark when wha' sud come in reet afore him but a laal women widout a heed. Ye may be sure he give' her grund fer agreement."

During the long winter nights of darkness, the families made sure they had enough wool spun into thread to be taken into Keswick for it to be woven into cloth.

"When t' threead and yarn was med, we took it doon to Keswick to owld Willy Dawson, or Billy Boow or Twentyman, and they weeved it for us into webbs o' cloth. It may be coarse wear, as they say, but it was gey substantial stuff, and kept yan rarely warm in winter. A good linsey woolsey skirt, and a short bed goon, was main o' t' dresses what t' lasses wear, wi black yarn stockin's and clogs." In Jollies Cumberland Guide and Directory of 1811, these three men were still in business in Keswick. Wm. Bow was listed as a weaver, as was Wm. Dawson, while J Twentyman was listed as a woollen manufacturer.

A record exists of a Mary Wilson who lived at Portinscale in 1794 recalling the occasions that she took wool to Keswick market. Although Mary was about 50 years older than Sarah, the market experiences of both would have been similar. Mary Wilson had need to be an extremely frugal woman for her whole earnings amounted to 2/6 a month, [twelve and a half pence] for carding and spinning 8 lbs of wool. *"She goes to Keswick regularly every four weeks with 8 lbs of yarn on her back and returns with 8 lbs of wool... Her time is thus employed, or in gathering fuel, viz; ferns, whins etc... Her dress is not expensive, her market going hat has served her thirty years, and her petticoat sixty five. Her pewter dishes are bright as when new, and her house neat and clean."* Mary paid fifteen shillings a year in rent for her house.

The common use of clothing made from Herdwick cloth with its long lasting properties indicates that Sarah Youdale's skin, as well as the many others like her, must have been much less sensitive to the irritating roughness of the wool, than modern day wearers of that material. Or is it just another illustration of how much more hardy were our forebears of 200 years ago.

Sarah's coarse workaday garments were exchanged on a Sunday for her best clothes of finer wool and linen, which had spent the week carefully folded away in an oak chest. Along with the other valley residents, Sarah enjoyed the opportunity to go to the small chapel, not only for the spiritual upliftment that it gave her, but to catch up on the local gossip. "There was some o' t' old statesmen as wadn't a' missed sarvice for nowt. They used to meet in t' chapel garth i' gey good time, an' git a' t 'news and mebbe hear of a stray sheep or two. Maistly too, their dogs cam wi' 'em. Owld Joss Harry, Ah can mind him niver missin', blaw high or blaw low."

Joss Harry came all the way over the tops from Watendlath for the Sunday service, and Sarah recalled that even after Joss Harry died and was buried, his dog still made the weekly journey to church to sit beside the old man's grave.

The church was the information centre of the valley for if there were ever any public notices to be given out, then this provided the opportunity. "If there was a sale gaan on, or owt public in t' deal, it was customary to mek it known efter folk had come out o ' t' chapel. Mebbe it wasn't reet, but folk dudn't think it so in them owld times."

Another opportunity for the dales folk to get together was when a wedding was held, and although there appears to be no evidence that Sarah ever married, she certainly enjoyed being "bidden" to a valley wedding, although these traditional Cumbrian weddings were dying out by the early part of the 19th century. "Ivverybody didn't mek such a deu...some stelt off d' ye know, an' git weddit an' niver a dog barked, an' nebody t' wiser 'til a' was over. But folk generally med a greet deu. There wad be as many as twenty, thirty gaan to t' kirk o' nag back; bride sittin' on a pillion aback o' her fadder. It was a varra cheerful sight to see them a' gaan doon t' road in a lang string on a fine summer mornin'.

After the service the newly married couple returned to the bride's home for the wedding dinner. "Efter dinner was ower, folk come frae a' parts o' t' deeal, an' bride sat in t'chair, in t' porch wid a wood dish on her knee. Ivverybody give her summat, an was pleased to give it; an' she wasn't shamed to tek it. An' a gey good thing it was to start life wid. But folk got ower prood to be behodden to yan anudder, an' Bidden Weddin's went oot o' fashion. There used to be wrustlin' an runnin', and lowpen in t' afterneun, an' plenty to eat and drink, and nowt nae worse."

The great celebration of the year for most people is Christmas, and it was no different for Sarah and her relatives and friends in the 18th and 19th century. Preparations are frantic enough in our appliance assisted lives, but for Sarah, the preparations for "Cursmass" began many months ahead of the great day itself, for their activities went on from Christmas to Candlemas. "It was a regular thing to brew in October fer Cursmass, an' some brewed seam time as t' cliippin."

Barley wine was a favourite brew, and some recipes still survive to produce the wishful sounding name of Cumberland brandy. Fermented liquid of many of the fruits of tree, hedgerow and vegetables from the field ensured that the spirit of Cursmass was celebrated with great merriment. Although the valley folk could supply most of their own needs for Cursmass fare, other necessities such as spices could only be obtained from one of the markets held in a larger town. Sarah dismissed Keswick market as being "nut mitch of a market. Borro'dle folk used to gaa ower t' Steak , an hire their sarvants an' sell their yarn at Hawkshead, but it was a lang way and a rough road, nut that they went mair than yance or twice a year...They went agean at Cursmass to sell their yarn and buy a lock o' spices wi' t' money to byak their pies, fer Cursmass were Cursmass then."

For the week before Cursmass, the activity intensified, for before the mutton pies could be baked, the sheep had to be killed. "For a' that week there was seck a scrows wi' killin sheep an' splittin' a' t'wood, an byakin' o' pies as niver was seen. Then on Yule lben, a gey gurt log was a back o' t' fire, an' t' barrel was tapped."

Sarah is reputed to have lived at Rosthwaite, just below Hazel Bank which is the fictitious home of Rogue Herries of Hugh Walpole's creation. The fireplace in her house was a huge open affair that could accommodate an enormous log, the end of which was left lying on the stone flags of the floor, and only pushed into the fire as new wood was needed. The log spluttered, the sparks flew and the heat warmed the room as only a well burning fire can. Families took great pride in choosing their yule log, it needed to be of such quality that it burned throughout the Cursmass season. It was considered to bring good fortune to a house if a Yule log could be lighted from the remains of that used the previous year. Huge fireplaces needed chimneys of character, and Sarah was proud of the chimney in her house. "A farmer's hoose didn't look amiss wid its gurt oppen chimley, full up t' rannel back wid hams an' flicks o' bacon an' legs o' mutton."

Card parties and visiting fiddlers turned each household into a whirl of activity over the Cursmass periods that Sarah could recall. "When Cursmass was fairly set in, we did nowt but feast an' dance an' play at cards til' Candlemas...we allus had a fiddler in t' deeal, an' there was niver a feast but what there was a dance... Yan fairly ran through yansel' at seck times; neet efter neet t' l yan wad gan off t' sleep next day amang yan' wark."

Hard work and hard play were constituents of Sarah Youdales's long life. As with most old people looking back over their lives, memories of the old days and ways always make their lifetimes seem so much better than that of the present generation. Sarah was no different from all our grandparents who see their early lives so much more disciplined and ordered than our own. 100 years ago, Sarah Youdale was decrying the qualities of the up and coming generation who fought in the Crimea, South Africa, the Somme and Ardennes. The old ones always think they know best!

Sarah Youdale died in her beloved Borrowdale in February, 1869, and was buried in the churchyard where her grave can still be seen. The letters on the stone have faded with age and encroaching lichens, but sufficient remains to identify the last resting place of Sarah Youdale, the Queen of Borrowdale.

IN
MEMORY OF
SARAH YOUDALE.
OF
ROSTHWAITE IN BORROWDALE
WHO DEPARTED THIS LIFE
FEBRUARY 23rd 1869
---- O ----
THE DECEASED WAS BORN IN BORROWDALE
WHERE SHE LIVED ALL HER LIFE AND DIED
UNIVERSALLY RESPECTED

Ben Pattinson with Sunset, a champion hound.

The start of a hound trail is known as the slip.

CHAPTER SEVEN

On the Trail of the Hounds

"Borrowdale allus was a strong spot for trail hounds", said Victor Brownlee of Stonethwaite Farm, who is now one of the most successful trainers in this popular Lake District sport. His name is a household word among the trailing fraternity, for he has bred and trained many champion hounds that include Shannon, Magnet and Miracle. All the names of Victor's hounds now begin with the letter M. "I don't really know how it came about, it just seemed to stick," he said. His reputation is such that enthusiasts come from far and wide to buy one of his dogs, or through involvement in a breeding programme, try to introduce some of his winning strain into their own hound's bloodline.

Hound trailing is a bit of a mystery to many visitors to the Lake District who may come across it for the first time at one of the valley shows. But these high profile trails are just the tip of the iceberg of the sport, for every season hundreds of trails are laid over fell and farm land to enable enthusiasts to send their dogs away. The hounds follow a trail that has been laid on the ground by two trailers who start from a central point, and return to a starting and a finishing line. The scent of the trail comes from a rag that has been well soaked in a mixture of aniseed and paraffin, and dragged over the circular course.

You need to be a real enthusiast to turn out in all sorts of weather conditions, there to wait anxiously for YOUR hound to return, hopefully yards ahead of the chasing pack.

Victor Brownlee is one such enthusiast. His interest in trailing began when he was a young lad, "My dad had one hound when we lived at Rosthwaite, but I really got going with Ben Pattinson who farmed at Longthwaite. He ran hounds for 35 years and he had some real champions among them. Now Ben had a wooden leg, but he could get anywhere on t' fells or t' crags. Wooden leg didn't stop him. He could get anywhere with that wooden leg."

Victor took Ben's hounds to some of the pre season practise trails and helped any of the other Borrowdale hound owners. "There was allus plenty of folk that would let me help out" so that by the time he acquired his own dog in 1969, Victor had picked up a wealth of information on hound trailing. But now with the benefit of many years of his own experience at the sport, he has come to the conclusion that there is no great secret to being a successful trainer. "It's all in the breeding. I maintain that mine are mostly decent because of the way they are brought up. Give them a good upbringing and you'll not go far wrong," he said. "Don't spoil them; they know who the boss is. It doesn't do to spoil them, though there's a lot that do."

Victor's first dog was called Shannon, and it was passed on to him by a couple of valley men who couldn't run it. Shannon proved to be one of Victor's most successful hounds and founded the strain from which all his other dogs have been bred. "Shannon, aye, it was the best un I had. It was an individual. It would get away on the trail and get out of sight of the rest of the pack, and that gave it an advantage. Once it got out of sight, the rest of the pack had to hunt the scent instead of following the lead dog."

Although most dogs can be regarded as pack animals, Victor likes his hounds to be individuals, to able to think for themselves. He explained that with foxhounds, which are heavier and built for stamina rather than speed, it is important that they hunt as a pack. "They need to act and hunt as a pack. One gives mouth and they're all there." A combination of speed, stamina and sense is what Victor is looking for in the hounds that he breeds. "These three S's are essential," he said." If you get one dog driving a race, the others will use it as a pacemaker. Some dogs are happy to do this, but a good dog will lead and then get clear out of sight."

One hound that had all these qualities would build up a massive lead and then when she was only ten or twenty yards away from the finishing line would sit there wagging her tail like mad, much to the dismay of the owner and any punter who had placed a bet on her. "It was almost as if she was saying, There I've done my job for the day. I've enjoyed myself. Can we go home? She was beaten many a time that way."

Victor now has the daughter of this hound. He calls he Michelle and described her as "a nice little bitch." Victor hopes she has not inherited her mother's bad habit of stopping short of the line. "I'll maybe have to keep her a bit short and hungry, to see how she goes. She'll maybe be keen to get to the bait box then."

Food is one of the key elements in the training programme of a hound dog. At one time each trainer had his own secret recipe for success which often ensured that the hounds were better fed than the trainer's family. Some recipes still survive for the special loaf that a trailer's wife would bake for her husband's dog to bring it to the peak of racing condition. The recipes included such ingredients as sherry, eggs, fruit, and vegetables. "There's still a few stick to the old ways," said Victor, "but feeding isn't the problem it used to be. At one time it was mainly flake maize with whatever meat or fish that you could get, but now these complete dog foods are OK. No dog should go short of food." Hounds are usually given their last big meal twenty four hours before they are due to run, so that they are "running hungry", although some trainers still give a breakfast of sherry and eggs on the day of the trail to "set them up" for the race.

Victor acknowledges that living in the Borrowdale valley gives him an advantage over many of the hound trail enthusiasts in West Cumbria where the sport has a strong following. When he goes "to the fell" to tend his sheep, he takes a couple of hounds with him. "I was gathering yesterday and took two young dogs with me. They see plenty when they're young; they learn the ground. They ran themselves 'til a standstill and enjoyed every minute. That's a terrific advantage; they learn to think for themselves when they're on the fell and it helps them when they're running trails. Likes o' them just has to get used to aniseed and that's it. You can do this when you're going to do your own work, but in the west most of the dogs have to be exercised on the lead."

The trails that the hounds follow are laid over farm, fell, and rough pasture land with the inevitable obstacles of gates, walls and wire fences. The promoters of a trail must ensure that the landowner gives permission for the dogs to run over private land and it is being recognised in many cases, this permission is not as easily forthcoming as was once the case. One outcome of this, that in Victor's opinion has become more noticeable over the last 10 years, is that there now seems to be more short trails organised. This may be because they do not require so many "permissions" to be obtained as with the longer trails. In some cases, changes brought about by land ownership, farming, or field letting can result in each field on a potential trail having a different owner. This situation presents a real headache for the promoter.

The trails are not measured by distance, but by the length of time it is estimated that it will take the hounds to cover the course. " Young hounds run trails of between 15 and 25 minutes and seniors run between 25 and 45 minutes. We seem to be getting more of these 26 minute trails now, but I prefer to see my hounds run for about 35 minutes." said Victor The difficulties presented by the terrain, or obstacles such as walls and fences all help to sort out the winners and the also rans.

The configuration of a trail hound is such that there is agility, strength, power and speed built into its lithely muscled frame. To watch a "slip " of trail hounds taking a low stone wall in an uninterrupted flowing stride is one of Lakeland's spectacles. The individual animals merge into a stream of colour; as a brown, white and black blur slides smoothly over the grey, mossed stones, before individual shapes emerge to stretch effortlessly into a long stride across a bracken covered slope. Higher walls demand a different technique; front broad pads seek a clambering purchase, while powerful haunches exert an upward thrust to send the hound clear of the wall.

It is inevitable that by running over rough and rocky ground, sun dried fields, and barbed wire fences, that these conditions will take their toll, thus resulting in some injuries to the dogs. Considering the number of animals that take part in the trails, there are relatively few serious injuries, although cuts and tears are common.. Many trailers feel that minor injuries are better left to heal naturally, relying on the dog's own tongue to provide the cleansing needed. "Hounds are usually very good healers, and a cut or tear can heal up very quickly. I feel that if a hound is taken to a vet every time it is cut, injections and antibiotics can lower its resistance to ailments. They're a bit like people; those that's allus running to a doctor seem to be forever badly."

Where possible, precautions are taken to minimise the risk of injury to the hounds when they are following a trail. Gates can be left open, barbed wire bagged at a crossing point and in many instances the wire may be tied down, but it is not uncommon to see hounds heading for a protected area of barbed wire, only to ignore that crossing and leap to either side. " They see something strange about ten or fifteen yards ahead, and they'll jump either side of it. They're only intent on going forward; they've no fear at all. Some o' t' visitors think it's cruel, but I'll say, they haven't a jockey on their backs to mek them run. They wouldn't run if they didn't enjoy it."

Trailing takes up a lot of Victor's time during the season that runs roughly from April to October. He has seven hounds in his kennels, "so there's always something to run." He aims to run each hound five times a fortnight, depending on the age of the hound, and the length of trail for which it is entered. "You don't want it to be doing three long trails in a week, so you slip in a short un to balance things out." He doesn't like to start running a young hound before it is fully developed, and claims if it is put to the aniseed too early, the trainer may be robbing the hound of its true potential. "But I do have the advantage of being able to let them run loose. These folk that start them off early, that have had them on a lead o' d time so they just run little bits o' short trails, so they have to start sooner than I do."

Victor is not the only member of the Brownlee family achieving success with the hounds, for his daughter Christine is a keen trailer, and his youngest daughter Helen also has her own two hounds. "Last year she was runner up in the Puppy Championship" said Victor, who sounded more pleased about his young daughter's success, than he did about his own. It was almost as an afterthought that he recalled some of his own achievements.

As a full time farmer with a large flock of sheep to care for, there are times when trailing has to be pushed into the background. " It's noticeable that when lambing time comes round, my hounds take a drop" he said. "You haven't time to put all into them that you should do. I've plenty to do then without hounds to bother about. You've to look after t' essentials."

Victor has recently been co - opted on to the executive committee of the Cumbrian Hound Trailing Association which was established in 1907, and is the body responsible for governing the sport in its own area. The Borders, North Yorkshire, North Wales and Ireland are other strongholds of the sport, and each has its own governing body. Prize money for winning animals is not very high, but entry fees, bookies fees and other moneys raised ensure there are large amounts to be distributed to worthy causes. "I feel quite strongly that people should be made aware of the financial contributions that hound trailing make to national and local charities" said Victor. "I don't think it is generally known that every year we give thousands of pounds to charities, like Cancer Research, local causes, and support small organisations in our own valleys or villages. Schools, old folks' groups, village halls, churches, institutes and such like all benefit from money raised by hound trailing."

Victor, Helen and Christine Brownlee

Tales of a Lakeland Valley - BORROWDALE

Peggy Horsley who formerly lived at Longthwaite Farm was one of the best of the women trailers. She is still a member of the Hound Trailing Association almost sixty years after she slipped her first hound. "But it's not the same when you're not involved with the hounds." Peggy began by helping her dad, Ben Pattinson, to walk his hounds. "We used to walk them three times a day. We'd let them run on the fells in winter, but dad really liked to walk them. And it didn't matter what time he finished work, and that could be late if we were hay timing, he would always give the hounds their massage afore he went to bed. Grease comes out of t' hounds when you rub them, and he massaged away til there was no more grease on his hands. There wasn't many that could massage them like he did; t' lisks were all pulled down and massaged. He massaged them twice a day, didn't matter what time he come in, hounds had to be massaged." That was Ben's way of keeping them supple, and an important part of his training programme.

Although Ben kept a few hounds of his own, it was as trainer of other peoples' hounds that established his reputation. "He had a lot of champions. Dairyman and Sunset won a lot of trophies between them." said Peggy. "The owners got the trophies, but dad had the satisfaction of training hounds that were champions three years in succession."

Peggy was able to explain how her dad, who was known to the farming community as Bap, lost his leg. "He got kicked playing football when he was only 12. He was in Carlisle hospital for 3 months and was devastated when he was told that his leg had to come off. He didn't care much what they did as long as he could still gaa to the fell. When he went to Newcastle to get his wooden leg, they couldn't understand why he wanted clinker nails in t' peg."

Peggy helped her dad not only with the hounds, but with shepherding and other farm work, and she once let him down on a rope to rescue a sheep that was fast on Gate Crag. "Rope was fastened til a tree mind, but I had to help him; there was no body else there. He had no fear of anything, and he nivver feared the fell. Anyway, we got that sheep up. But he could do owt wid that wooden leg."

The nature of farming in the Borrowdale valley has changed dramatically in the last sixty years. Peggy Horsley recalled that two horses were kept on Longthwaite Farm to help with ploughing, mowing, turning and scaling. "We had one field below Rosthwaite and dad used to go early morning before sun got up; it was better for t' horses sake, really. Scaler had prongs in it to scale the hay." The use of the valley fields have changed over the years. "You don't see hay timing now not like it used to be; it was a great thing was hay timing it really was a jolly time." Some of the valley hay fields have now become swampy areas.

"We used to keep cattle; ours were all Shorthorns, but you don't see them nowadays. We used to get our milk straight from cow, it wasn't cooled or owt and it never did us any harm. We made our own butter. We grew all our own potatoes and vegetables, we were self sufficient really, although our tatie field was away past t' school." Peggy recalled that when potatoes were required for meals for the family, or any visitors that were staying at the farm, she was dispatched on her bike, to the "tatie field" to lift them fresh from the ground. "I'd to gaa on t' bike wid a bucket and dig for t' taties."

On her parents farm, there was a day for every activity around the farmhouse. Monday was always washing day, when the water in the set pot was heated to boil the clothes.

"Thursday was churning day. We had one churn with a handle at each side and it needed two on you to turn it, that was like a barrel. Then we got an end over end churn, that was more modern." Two pigs were kept every year to be killed and the meat cured to provide hams, bacons, black puddings and sausage. It was reckoned that everything on a pig could be used apart from its grunt!

Foxes caused something of a problem among the hens as Peggy recalled. " When snow was on the ground, you could see that a fox had been about. One mornin' when Ah went to see to t' hens, it had worried the lot; 23 Ah think there was. They hadn't been shut up, and it had gone with the lot. They were lyin' all t' field over. Ah said, ah wouldn't a' cared if it had gone wid what it wanted, but no, it had worried the lot. They just do it for fun, ah would say."

There was also the ongoing problem of foxes attacking lambs, and when this became a major problem, the hunt was called in to try and deal with the fox. "George Bell was huntsman when dad was farming. He used to gaa before it was leet, dad wasn't varra keen about that really but Geordie often had a fox killed by six o' clock."

Most trailers keep their hounds outdoors in barns, sheds or kennels and Bap Pattinson was no exception, but Peggy found that once they were allowed in the house, for one reason or another, it was a terrible job to get them to live outside again. "Dairyman had to have an operation on his ear, a great lump o' cartilage had been taken out. When bandage come off there was blood ivverywhere. I said, I'll tek him up home. Father said, you'll nivver manage him. But I said, I will. I nivver slept that night. I med him a bed beside me, and I huggled his foot in case he moved. He was alright; it took a bit, but I couldn't get him out of the house after that."

Peggy learned a lot about hounds and trailing from her dad and when both her dad and her husband died within 12 days of each other, she reckoned that it was her hound Mick that was the saving of her. "His running name was Buchail, It's Irish for Boy, and he went on to win the championship three years in succession. He was born in 1974, a son of Victor Brownlee's great hound , Shannon. He just came at the right time for me. Lads in t' valley couldn't do anything with him. They put him in t' pack for a while, in t' Blencathra, to quieten him down because he got a bit nasty, but that was before Ah got him. Mind Ah'd some fights wid him before Ah got him to gaa."

Peggy recalled the first time she slipped Mick in a practice trail at Loweswater. "There was 70 odd hounds slipped, and he won. An' then we took him to Troutbeck, at Windermere. There was 70 odd in that trail an' he won that. He was marvellous with me was Mick, and he lived with me; he was just like a human. Ah used to bath him and used Amplex shampoo, it hed a lovely smell. Ah used to bath him out there in a big zinc bath. When he got out, he was just like a human being, he would step out and put one paw on til a towel, and then t' other, and then give his sel' a shek. He was marvellous was Mick. We just seemed to hit it off."

Mick went on to win many trails for Peggy, "he did the double at Grasmere", and he established such a reputation that he was actually used in a television advertisement for dog food. "We had to go down Sea'waite and set him to, jumping walls. They couldn't get it right. He was sick, and Ah was sick as owt. They seemed to want to do t'same thing over and over again. Poor dog, he was supposed to eat all this food. They did it so many times that he was absolutely pig sick of it. I'd to keep putting bits o' chocolate in his dish to mek it look as though he was eatin' the meat."

Buchail made another celebrity appearance, but this time at Crufts, the prestigious dog show. Peggy was reluctant to let him go to where he was to take part in the parade of champion dogs. "Ah didn't gaa wid him, and Ah was in such a state. When they went, there was a tune playin' on t' wireless, There Goes My Only Possession." The words of the song almost came true, for Peggy described how the dog escaped at Crufts and was only recaptured by a huntsman before he got clean away. Much to Peggy's relief Buchail was safely returned.

Peggy was a familiar figure at trails for many years in her red jacket and earned herself the nickname "The Lady in Red." "I took to wearing the red jacket after attending a trail at Winscales. Our dog wasn't in the first six; six had gone up to git their tickets, and Mrs Sim, she went up wid hers, and she'd a red jacket on, an' our dog saw her red jacket afower he saw me. So Ah said, they needn't say they're colour blind, cos he noticed red jacket and so I allus took to wearing red after that. And that was Dairyman in 1961."

Peggy acknowledges that there's nothing like the excitement of slipping your own hound and waiting for it coming back. "Mind you, it used to mek me feel fair badly waiting for him coming back in case owt had happened to him, wondering if he would be torn, where some of them don't seem to bother, do they."

Some of the trails caused Peggy concern because of the height of the fences that the dogs had to jump. "We once went to Westward, and I was worried sick cos there's some awful fences down there. But they said he'll be alright, and Victor's hound had won it week before. When Ah saw them fences near t' finish, it med me feel quite ill, really. But anyhow, Mick took them no bother, he won; he beat Victor's that had won week afore."

Peggy Horsley. The cabinet contains some of her many hound trailing trophies

CHAPTER EIGHT

Power to the Valley

Visitors and even those who now live in Borrowdale, take very much for granted the flick of a switch that brings instant power to house, hotel or farm. Mains electricity has swept even remote valleys into the hurly burly of late 20th century life with the advent of freezers, automatic washing machines, televisions, cleaners and cookers, to mention but a few.

Mains electricity came into the Borrowdale valley in the 1960's when trenches were dug to enable the power carrying cables to be discreetly hidden below the ground. It wasn't until 1978, that electricity was brought to Watendlath for the big switch on. Farmer Dick Richardson remembered the exact day; "Electricity come to Watendlath on the 19th of December 1978. We had a Christmas Tree on t' car park that was lit up t' 1 March."

What was life like in those pre - electric days?

David Tyson who has lived at Watendlath all his life needed no prompting. "It was bloody awful , I can tell you," he said. David lives at Stepps End Farm, the first one encountered as the hamlet is approached by the road from Ashness.

The earliest form of lighting that he could remember was that used by his family when they lived in John Green House Farm, now renamed Fold Head Farm. "It was Aladdin oil lamps. T'old lass had like an enamel tea pot widout a lid. She went in t' barn theer many a time to t' drum o' paraffin. Many a hundred times she's filled teapot full o' paraffin for t' old Aladdin's." David recalled that as soon as four o' clock came it was time to start filling up the lamps, and it was the use of these Aladdin lamps that led to many a fire in the Watendlath farms and cottages. "In t' middle house there, in t' kitchen" said David, "in t' main oak beam about half way along, there's a square bit chiselled out where t' lamp set beam a fire. On'y way they could stop it was to git hammer and chisel, and chisel it out. Wood was that hard, they couldn't wet it; they were hevin' to throw watter up all t' time." Most of the buildings that still remain at Watendlath have a substantial part of their structure and fabric dating back to the 17th century, and their low, blackened oak timber beams are as hard as stone.

One of the most serious fires resulted in loss of life about 1876. "T' auld fella that lived there had been to Stonethwaite to see somebody, and he was coming back ower t' fell, be t' larch trees there, and he saw house had been burned down and his housekeeper was burned to death." said David. The true cause of that fire was never ascertained. "The bricks stood there for many years, but it just got gradually worse and worse."

David explained that the Aladdin lamps were only used in the main living areas, and had to be carefully maintained with their cotton wicks neatly trimmed , otherwise the black smoke darkened the glass and the benefit of the light was lost. As far as upstairs lighting was concerned, "well we took candles up to bed wid us" said Dick.

Eventually, paraffin lamps and candles gave way to Calor gas. "Tommy Walker frae Keswick put it in" said Dick. "Pipes was put all through t' houses. It was a helluva thing was that gas. There was two laal chain things hanging down frae t' lights and you just hed to pull them to put t' leet on and off."

The earliest form of electricity that was used in Watendlath was that powered by their own generator, which was driven by a Coventry Climax engine; but it only proved sufficient energy to light up one or two of the houses. David Tyson recalled those early attempts to brighten Watendlath in the years following the second world war. "They had their own generator in t' bothy house theer. There's a Coventry Climax engine in t' turbine house; they used them on t' search lights in t' war. I dunno how they got amang it like. We'd leet off it though, but it was just a trial run over Christmas. They put so much petrol in t' engine to see how lang it would last. I can't just remember; nobbut two or three minutes for a pint o' petrol. We'd lights on ower Christmas, then t' idea was scrapped."

A more efficient means of creating on site electricity arose when "Old" John Bailey, an official of the Planning Board met some of the Watendlath men. "We got tergither ya day, talkin' to see if they couldn't work summat out wid watter. Ya thing led til another, then our John went to Skelt Robinson at Thirlmere for some sheep ya morning. He nivver come back; he nivver come back; we couldn't tell what had gan wrong."

John had taken the opportunity to talk to some of the Thirlmere folk about a turbine at the Thirlmere Dam project, that had supplied them with electricity before they were switched on to the mains. "It charged up this room full o' batteries and give them a bit o' leet. We med enquiries of Manchester Water Works and finished up buying it. Derwent went with t' old David Brown [tractor] from Middle Row; and me and John frae here, I dunno who else. We were reet in under t' dam gittin' that greet thing out o' theer. I rode on t' tractor wid Derwent up Soapery Brow; what a weight was that. T' old David Brown was near up in t' air. Any way we come up here, knocked wa' down to t' turbine house. It was built, but roof was nut on it. We crow barred her down, t' generator of t' tractor, and put roof on t' turbine house."

The turbine driven by the water power just below the fall known as the Punchbowl, provided electricity for Watendlath until mains electricity was installed in 1978. "It was a great thing when it was gaan" said Dick, "and it was gaan til lectric come. It was all right as lang as it rained and there was plenty o' watter in the beck."

Winter brings short days and long dark nights to a valley that is completely encircled by mountains and before the installation of a mains electricity supply, the battery powered wireless could be regarded as the only source of commercial entertainment. Even that had to be used sparingly to conserve the power in the batteries. "They used to just listen to t' wireless didn't they; and then only news and we hadn't to mek a sound," said David. He recalled coming home from school one day to find a "damn square thing sitting theer. We didn't know what it was, but it was a wireless. Saturday night, we all had to be quiet while they git football results."

Saturday was an important day as far as the wireless was concerned, for that was the day that the batteries were taken into Keswick to Harry Denwood's shop near the Alhambra Cinema. There they were left to be put on charge and collected the following week. David's family sent their batteries in by trap , while Dick recalls that they used to go from High Lodore farm on the Borrowdale bus. "We used to have them in a laal joiner med box and they would gaa on the bus. Laal Harry Denwood would charge 6 pence. You had to fetch charged uns back. You daren't fergit. There was a helluva row if batteries was flat."

David Tyson's father and brothers at Watendlath in 1940, when even the dog had his own gas mask

Shaun Richardson, David Tyson and Dick Richardson reminisce over old photographs in Fold Head Farm kitchen.

Tales of a Lakeland Valley - BORROWDALE

The way in which the inhabitants of Watendlath spent their long winter evenings was a source of puzzlement to some council workers who were digging the trench for the electricity supply. David Tyson stopped to have a crack with some of them. "Fellas had been discussing what we did up theer at nights. Just then, t' van pulled up, full wid all t' kids frae skeul. Ah, yan o them workmen sed , Noo Ah see what tha does of a neet."

Dick Richardson repeated the tale that old Jont Hinde who used to live at Stonethwaite told about the 13 families that lived at Watendlath. "There was once 13 families up there, and there was 13 pregnant women all at the same time. It was a fella that used to gaa round working like."

"He had been working all right , hadn't he? " was David Tyson's comment.

Fold Head Farm where Dick Richardson lives has changed its name over the years, and between 1944 and 1980 was known as John Green House Farm, which may have been a reference to a John Green who lived in Watendlath during the 19th century. It was under that name when David Tyson lived there with his parents. David's memory of the farm goes beyond that of Dick, for he can recall the time when it was home for two families. The present comfortable kitchen with its heavy black beams, was once the wash house. "There was just a big set pot there" said David, pointing to an alcove. "On washing day, they would use caustic soda. One laal lass drunk some caustic soda out o' t' white enamel ladling pan. It shrivelled her stomach up and she hungered to death. They took her to doctor at Edinburgh, but there was nowt that he could do; it was ower late." Dick Richardson also had experience of caustic soda which he described as " fearful stuff. I remember caustic soda. We used to scrub flags wid it to git them cleaned off." Most of the valley farms had their floors covered with rectangular flags of stone, and these still remain in many of the farm houses

Cooking and baking were done on a huge iron range that filled most of one wall of a kitchen, and was demanding of a constant source of fuel. "When t' visitors were in and we were mekin' Yorkshire puddin's for t' dinner, well t' oven hed to be red hot for that, hedn't it. Then t' shout wad gaa up, Dry oven wood, and summat wad 'ev to git chopped."

"A helluva thing was y'oven wood, " commented Dick. "Ay y'oven wood; great lang lengths of it . It had to be dry as weel. You shoved it underneath t' flue. There was t' old dampers on top o' t' range as weel for cleanin' t' oven out."

Television was late coming to the valley and even now the quality of reception is very varied. Dick reckons "its nothing much to shout about", while David appreciates the fact that his farmhouse is better placed to receive a signal from a booster station. "Aunty decided we would have a television set sent frae Hetherington's o' Cockermouth. John Dawson come that used to be t' postman. He got thing set up and went to put aerial on top o' t' hill where there's two great steans. He thowt we should git a good picture from theer. He went up t' hill; and there was not a squeak. Only spot we could get a picture was with t' aerial in t' rowan tree aside kitchen window."

One of the characters that was well known to both David and Dick was Vivian Fisher who used to be guardian of a gate on the Watendlath road, just before the steepness of the road levels out to Ashness Bridge. He was a tall, lean man with a tanned weather beaten face and balded head. His long straggly white hair marked him as a sort of eccentric, before the style became as acceptable as it is today. He manned the gate from about Easter until the end of October and performed the service of opening and closing

49

it for cars and walkers. He never refused the few coppers that were dropped into his extended hand.

This was not the only gate on the Watendlath road, for Dick Richardson recalled, "When Ah worked at Eshness there was a gey lock o' yats up here. There was 13 o' them between Watendlath and t' road end. Ah used to gaa down wid a load o' muck to them fields at Barra House and fetch a load o' keal back and it took all bloody day. We used to put muck out in heaps, then gaa to t' lake to wesh t' cart out, cut keal in next field and fetch it up. Keal was for t' beasts. We fothered them in t' bark barn. Gates! Bloody nuisance they were; on'y good for firewood."

Vivian chose his gate well, for it was on one of the steep parts of the road that branches up from the Borrowdale valley. There were no cattle grids to prevent animals straying on to the main valley road; the gates kept them enclosed. Many motorists were only too pleased to avoid an awkward halt on the steep, narrow road, and thus escape the need to leave their vehicle in order to open and close the gates. Alan Mounsey of Grange recalled the problem that Vivian had in closing a gate before the arrival of the next car. "He would say; Ah have sek a job at times to git t' yat shut afore next poor car comes up."

Very few passed Vivian by without giving him some money, and there was always a gap toothed smile, and a polite word to see them on their way. "If they didn't give him anything, he called them Cockneys," recalled one valley man, "but never to their face!" Some of those who walked along the road took the opportunity to stay awhile with Vivian, as he whistled for birds to come down from the holly and ash trees to perch on his sun tanned arms that protruded from his rolled up shirt sleeves. Chaffinches and blue tits, great tits and robins as well as the bold blackbird used to come to be fed with crumbs from his cloth covered wicker basket. The birds showed no fear of Vivian, or anyone else for that matter, as long as they stayed quiet and still.

At the end of the day, when there seemed to be no more cars travelling the valley road, Vivian would gather his belongings and set off for the walk back to his Keswick cottage. Sometimes he was fortunate to get a lift. "Ya day, we give him a lift into Keswick and t' pockets o' that bloody old coat he used to wear were fair hangin' down below his knees, wid money." Each morning, Vivian took his previous days takings to two shops in Keswick, to change the coppers. "He would tek about 5/- in small change and that was a lot o' money then He was an old fella when Ah knew him" said Dick. "I think he was about 90 when he died."

Vivian was in fact 93 when he died in on April 3 1976. He was born in Leyton's Yard, Keswick in 1883, and grew up as a member of a large family. As soon as he was old enough to start work, he became a postman, and walked tremendous distances delivering the mail. He served in the 1914 - 18 war, and after being wounded, a stay in the notorious transit camp of Etaples in France, is said to have changed his values and outlook on life. Although he had a humble upbringing, he was a great collector of china, books and pictures, he read extensively and admired the works of the Lakes poets and writers, and he was himself an accomplished painter. Vivian was one of the townsfolk who attended the funeral of John Ruskin.

CHAPTER NINE

A Valley in Trust

The National Trust's symbol of the oak leaf is especially appropriate in Borrowdale, for the beautiful river Derwent that rises in Sprinkling Tarn and enters the sea at Workington, takes its name from the old Celtic word "dawr", meaning oaks. At one time, the river certainly did flow through the valley of the oaks, but over the years, the activities of charcoal burners, wood cutters and the browsing of many generations of sheep have taken their toll. There is little of the indigenous woodland left behind, but in Great Wood and Johnny's Wood, both of which are owned by the National Trust, there are still reminders of what these woodlands were like.

The National Trust owns about a quarter of the Lake District National Park, and this makes it one of the major land owners. Much of that land is in the Borrowdale valley, where the first purchase was made in 1902 when Canon Rawnsley, who was for many years Vicar of Crosthwaite, helped to raise enough money from public subscription to buy Brandlehow, on the western shore of Derwentwater. Some six years later, 107 acres of wood, park and rough land just south of Brandlehow was bought by the Trust. Canon Rawnsley was one of three people who helped to found the National Trust.

As well as being a principal landowner in the Borrowdale valley, the National Trust is a major employer and counts among its workforce many local people who are employed in woodland, tourism, and conservation projects. Mike Roulson of Stonethwaite is the head warden of the National Trust in Borrowdale. " I didn't know the valley intimately when I began work here 10 years ago, but by gum, I soon found out. I had to, because of the size of the area, and the responsibilities I was taking on." Mike looks on the 25,000 acres that is under his charge as his "back garden", which includes not only the valley land [excluding woodland], but fell land that extends to Scafell Pike and Great Gable.

"The beauty of the job is that you never know what's going to happen. I can have a diary of events, then the phone rings and the day is changed completely. No two days are ever alike."

Mike's job can be compared with that of the manager of a large estate and as such, brings a necessary amount of paper work. Budget control, work programmes and planning are all aspects of his job, but there are plenty of occasions when he leaves the paper mountains on his desk to escape to the real heights of the fells. "Obviously you can't run this sort of an area from behind a desk; you've got to be out a lot to see the problems." Mike often leaves his paper work for a wet day and as he pointed out, "Living in Stonethwaite, we get plenty of those."

Mike works very closely with Borrowdale's tenant farmers, for apart from three farms, all the rest are owned by the National Trust. "Over the years, upland farming has declined and many farmers now work single handed, or with a son to help. The Trust can help them out by supplying man power to carry out some of the tasks that need to be done."

Tales of a Lakeland Valley - BORROWDALE

Mike has a team of two other full time wardens, a two man estate team, a four man footpath team, two car park attendants as well as an army of volunteers to help out with maintenance and improvement work on fell and farm land. Valuable conservation work has been carried out under Trust direction by teams of unemployed people from West Cumbria. Hedging, walling, footpath repair work, maintenance of stiles and gates, ditching, and drainage work are just some examples of the necessary work carried out by Mike's team of full time workers and volunteers.

Acorn Camps provide another source of voluntary help. These are held all over the country at different National Trust properties, and there are usually two each year in Borrowdale where they are based at the Bowder Stone bothy. "People come from all over the country. They arrive on Saturday not knowing each other, but by Sunday, they are all good buddies," said Mike. Another National Trust bothy at Watendlath is also an ideal base for volunteers to spend what amounts to a working holiday. The bothy is well equipped and can accommodate up to 12 people who can stay for any length of time. "Some volunteers come for two or three days, others come for two or three months. Some have stayed for as long as six months. We can teach them a lot of skills in that time," said Mike. Along with the comfortable accommodation, the volunteers have the use of a vehicle and after putting in an eight hour day working for the National Trust, the rest of the time is their own. Mike pointed out the value of this type of voluntary help, for as pre-booking is essential, he knows exactly the scale of help that is available and how he can put it to the best use.

The whole of the Watendlath valley belongs to the National Trust and tenant farmer Dick Richardson has farmed at Fold Head Farm since 1972. "Years ago, I can remember there used to be three working farms here, with nine men working on them, an' they were allus doing some kind of job or other. It's nearly all sheep now, there's not a big lot o cattle." he said. Dick is one of a dying generation of farmers who remembers working with horses. "They tried to larn me to plough when I was 14, but I wasn't strang enough to hod stang and hosses togither, because on them swing ploughs there was no wheels. When I lifted them up, plough went into t' grund and the bloody hosses near come up. And then they shouted, Press down on t'stangs lad, so I pressed doon on t'stangs and the bloody plough shot out o' t' grund." He did eventually learn to handle the plough and commented that "efter we're gone, there'll nut be a man jack left that can gear up a hoss to work."

Years ago, lengths men were employed to look after a particular stretch of road. It was their responsibility to maintain the road's surface, to clear the drainage channels and gutters, and to infill any holes that developed. The National Trust have re introduced this concept in Borrowdale where there is now a team of eight volunteers who have taken on the responsibility of keeping an eye on some of the valley footpaths, over twenty of which have been repaired by traditional pitching methods. "You can't just repair a path and walk away from it and think you never need look at it again." said Mike. "You've got to keep culverts clear, and remove stone debris otherwise the pitching gets completely covered up. These lengths men are now providing a valuable service."

The ability to communicate with people and enjoy good working relationships with the valley farmers and his own staff is a vital part of Mike's job. He is seen in the valley as the representative of the National Trust and as such, realises the responsibility that this carries. "I've to be seen as someone who can be trusted to keep my word. If I don't think something's right, I'll tell 'em; and if there is a genuine complaint, I'll take it on board and try and resolve it."

Tales of a Lakeland Valley - BORROWDALE

Borrowdale is probably one of the most visited of the Lake District valleys and as a major land owner, the National Trust has the responsibility of helping to manage the influx of visitors and repair some of the damage they leave behind them. "It's a wish of mine that people will respect the area," said Mike. "There are some who come up here and look upon it as a National Park owned by the nation, and feel that it is free for them to do exactly as they please. That is a fallacy. It's not owned by the nation. The Lake District receives millions of visitors every year and if only a small percentage leave litter and cause damage, it still comes to a considerable amount. They don't seem to realise that somebody has to pick up the litter; somebody has to put out their fires. Some people arrive thinking the Lake District is one huge camp site."

Mike explained that usually a quiet, tactful word is all that's needed to move campers on to the official sites, or persuade them to douse their barbecue fires. "There's no point in aggravating people," he said. "Most people are quite good about it. It's a slow process of educating people as to what's right, and what's wrong for the area."

An Information Centre at the boat landings at Derwentwater is an obvious advantage to visitors; car parks have been provided at Great Wood, Watendlath and Seatoller, while a recent introduction has been a mini bus service to Watendlath. This has changed a former nightmare drive along a narrow, steep walled road, into a pleasant journey with an opportunity to enjoy the scenery on the way to the remote hamlet.

Mike's colleague in managing Borrowdale for the National Trust is David Thomason who is the head forester in the valley. He has the responsibility of managing 1500 acres of actual woodland, their enclosing 35 miles of wall and fencing, as well as keeping a watchful eye on the rest of the trees that belong to the National Trust in the valley. "That's trees on fell sides as well as those on tenanted land." He has a small team of 3 men to help him, "The Trust are feeling the pinch the same as everyone else. It gets harder and harder; we just have to shove jobs back."

Most of the jobs that David and his team have to do need the hands on approach, from the weeding and control of undergrowth, to the felling of mature timber. "We use chain saws, and always work in pairs," said David. Much of the work they do goes unnoticed by visitors to the Lakeland valley and that's the way that David likes it. "If the changes were obvious we wouldn't be doing our job right," he said. "A forester has always to be looking well ahead, as much as 100 years. You need to plant trees that are going to need replacing well ahead of one's own lifetime. There's some lovely birches at Ashness Bridge and with the lifespan of a birch about 100 years, the trees that are there now are about 60, so we need an ongoing programme of underplanting to make sure that it stays one of the best views in the Lake District."

David loves trees, especially Scots pine and oak, but feels no regrets when some of the ancient timber has to be felled. "I love trees, but I'm realistic enough to know that they are going to die eventually, and the best thing you can do with a tree is to utilise it and plant another in its place. You're using it gently for the value of the community. You're not actually destroying the countryside, you're keeping it ticking over basically."

What attracts David to trees, "Well they're great big things; they attract wildlife and they look great in the landscape." Flat topped Scots pine, ancient yews and oaks, even the gnarled and wind shaped larches help to give character to the valley in Trust. "They just set the landscape off; they are part of the scene. Its a question of balance; we are trying to balance conservation with public access and the aesthetic qualities of landscape, and trying to make a little bit of money to help pay for all this."

Trees are felled in Borrowdale for a variety of reasons, often it is to break up the age structure of the woodland. David explained that this means the woodlands are almost self sustaining for as older trees die off, there are younger ones coming through to take their place. "In an ideal world you wouldn't have to do anything for as an old tree dies and falls down, it creates a gap in the canopy that lets sunlight in and a new tree would come through to take its place, but it doesn't work that way with sheep grazing. Sheep are the bane of my life! I must say, its not as bad as it used to be."

A number of big trees are sold as a "standing sale" , and this is usually put out to tender. "We also have to fell for safety reasons, especially with the Dutch Elm disease. If they are on the road side or near a car park, they get the chop; it's too dangerous to leave them standing. When they are too big for us to handle, we get the contractors in. You need specialised machinery for some jobs that we don't have."

There is little replanting of the woodland in Borrowdale for David explained they are trying to encourage natural regeneration. "What we are trying to do is to retain the genetic stock of the valley, although it has been heavily modified over centuries, except in the ghylls. and some of the inaccessible crags" Only about 800 trees were planted in 1995 and these were mainly conifers to retain a source of income and supply the Trust with wood for their own purposes. own purposes by for fences and building timbers. "As far as possible we like to be self sufficient in timber. and to do that you need to plant conifers." Oak timber is sometimes needed for repair work on Trust properties in situations where it has been used in the past. "Where it is riven timber, then we do rive by hand. We do it to order, roof beams, joists, and we need to go out looking for trees that we can get the timber off. We've got to get them felled, get them back to the mill, then rive by hand and cut to size, so its quite a long slow process that is very labour intensive. Riving is splitting the timber with hammer and wedges, and then using an adze to actually finish it off and clean it up. and get it to as near the size as we can. The timber goes in green, that's the way it used to go in, and this is where you get the lovely wavy effects on old roofs. When you first put the roof in it looks quite straight but as the timbers move and warp and twist, you start getting the movement in the roof."

It's not only the National Trust joiners that are supplied with Borrowdale oak, for it is sold privately to different parts of northern England to be used in old buildings where timbers need to be replaced. "It's a specialised market, and there's not many people can afford it" he commented. "It's got to be high quality trees although they don't need to be a big ones. We've gone back to the old ways and now we pick a tree that fits the size of the job we have to do."

Most of David's management work is concerned with conservation of woodland, amenity woodland which allows public access, and landscape. "Commercial forestry comes a long, long way down the list." Some of the conservation woodland has very little intervention done to it; in such cases, nature is allowed to take its course. Where there is public access to woodland, safety work is a priority for compaction of the ground in a woodland car park can cause root damage of the trees, which leads to die back and the inevitable safety problems. "They've a hard life these old trees".

The trees in the great Wood car park have some of the best lichens in the valley in spite of the attentive activities of nuthatches trying to get at the insects underneath. The nuthatch is only one of about 50 species that are regularly to be found in the valley and David combines his own hobby of ornithology with the Trust policy of encouraging birds to nest in the woodland. "We encourage species like pied flycatcher, redstart and tree pipit just by keeping the sheep grazing in some of the woods to keep the close cropped vegetation that most birds like. We also put nest boxes up and are always aware of leaving non intervention woodland for the wildlife. Places like Ings Wood which is one of the Sites of Special Scientific Interest"

None intervention of woodland allows certain areas to go through the natural process of growth, die back, fall and rot to allow recycling of nutrients to take place. Even some of the natural looking woodland has been coppiced or pollarded in years gone by and it is part of the management plan to continue this where appropriate.

Increase of visitors number throughout the year has made life rather more difficult for carrying out some forestry jobs such as roadside tree surgery. "The hazard is there all the time, but the risk increases with the number of people who happen to be there. There's no close season for visitors as there used to be. There's always people knocking about, especially at week ends, and that makes things a bit difficult. But generally, people are much better than they used to be. You don't find them parking in gateways now, and obstructing places of work. I think the public are becoming more aware and better educated as far as the countryside is concerned."

The major hazard to a forester is fire. In the hot, dry summer there is a constant state of alert to make sure that small fires illegally lit by campers do not get out of control and spread through tinder dry woodland. "Some of them will light a fire at the base of a tree, and that damages the tree as well as presenting a fire hazard." The flames, or even the reflected heat can actually damage the tree by boiling the sap in the wood which ruptures all the cells that supply the nutrients, and the tree will die on that side. Once the bark comes off, it can let fungus and all kinds of disease in, so fires can result in all sorts of problems. We've lost quite a few trees on the islands that way, and then we have to fell them for other people's safety then." The woodlands are home to a good mammal population in the valley which includes badgers, foxes, and red squirrels. After a slow and steady growth in squirrel numbers, 1995 saw a reduction. Post mortem results on some of those found sick or dead revealed bronchitis to be the cause. "There's plenty of stoats and weasels about so they are doing well"

If David is concerned about the appetites that valley sheep display for young trees, he is prepared to tolerate the 60 strong herd of deer that have moved into the Borrowdale valley from Thirlmere. "The stags can do a lot of damage to a tree by rubbing the velvet from their antlers. They damage the bark and that lets disease in to the tree. I like red deer" he said, "but they can make a mess of a plantation. We've had roe deer ever since I've been here 24 years, they do a little bit of damage marking their territory and so on but now we're getting the reds from Thirlmere, and when they're getting the velvet off their antlers they do make a mess."

During the summer the antlers of a red deer stag are covered with a soft velvet like substance, but once the antler is full grown, the stags rub their antlers against trees to remove the soft covering to reveal the hard, "bone like" substance below.

"They knock the bark off and that lets damage in. They make a mess of my walls as well, especially round Ashness wood where they jump on top of the walls and cause gaps. If that was sheep I'd be going mad, but deer, I 'm quite laid back about it."

Being close to wildlife is one of the perks of the job as far as David is concerned; it almost makes it an extension of his interest in natural history. He is keen to record sightings and changes in the wildlife population of the valley. "Little things like seeing a red necked phalarope on the lake, watching the resurgence of the peregrines, and even the spread of kestrels into the valley," are all noted. " We never use to see a kestrel above Grange, ever, but they're up Langstrath now."

Part of David's job involves taking parties round woodland, talking to groups of interested people, and informing high powered conferences of the National Trust's woodland management policy. David is quite a laid back character, but even he was "slightly phased" at one London Conference when he spotted Sir David Attenborough sitting in the third row!

Conservation, amenity access, woodland management and education are the corner-stones of his job. "If we invite the public into our woodlands, they have to be safe places" he said.

Membership of the National Trust brings advantages both to the Trust and the member. It provides much needed income from subscriptions, aided by bequests and legacies to provide the essential finances to manage the properties owned, "in the best interests of the Nation." For the member, there is not only free access to Trust properties, but the satisfaction of knowing that a contribution is being made to preserving and conserving some of the finest scenery in the country.

David Thomason who is head forester of the National Trust in Borrowdale, keeps an eye on the valley wildlife, as well as the trees

Borrowdale is still a working valley, and the birches at Ashness are under constant review to ensure this famous view retains its character

Footpath repair work can be hard, cold and wet!

CHAPTER TEN

When Eagles Flew in Borrowdale

"It's an eagle" goes up the cry from behind a pair of binoculars that are trained on a soaring bird with broad wings, that rises high on summer thermals above the Borrowdale valley. Well, he could be right, but its 99% more likely that the circling bird that causes the excitement is more likely to be a buzzard, one of the Lake District's most common birds of prey.

Actual and confirmed sightings of eagles in the Lake District are comparatively few in these modern times although a pair of eagles have bred with varied success in the Haweswater valley for over 20 years. That is no distance at all from Borrowdale as the eagle flies. Riggindale is only 18 kilometres due east from Borrowdale's Eagle Crag and this Haweswater valley is currently favoured by England's only pair of nesting golden eagles. During the 1970's another pair of eagles bred sporadically in the west of the county and there are occasional sightings in southern Lakeland valleys of what are probably passage birds moving between England and Scotland. In recent years, eagles have been spotted in almost every major Lake District valley, at one time or another. My personal encounters range from a magical few seconds when a huge bird hung on the wind only about twenty feet above my head, to a sighting of an eagle soaring with nine buzzards over Bassenthwaite Lake. Distance is as nothing to these huge birds, and a flick of the wings into a powerful glide can send it into distance and another valley .

The present record of eagle sightings in the Lake District is a meagre state of affairs when compared to about two hundred years ago; for then eagles were once a common sight soaring over the mountains of the Lake District . It led to a saying of "an eagle for every mountain", although this is an exaggeration, for a pair of these huge birds need an extensive area of land over which to hunt in order to obtain food to feed themselves and their young. If the sort of detailed recording which is now a feature of ornithological monitoring had been applied , it may even then have only yielded half a dozen pairs of eagles nesting in the Lake District, but the impression is given that sightings of eagles were more common and the population more numerous, than it is today.

One has only to study the maps of the Lake District to realise that the many Eagle Crags that are to be found, denote that at one time, the largest British bird of prey made its home in the Lakeland mountains. This was in spite of attempts to rid the Lake District of a bird that was classed along with other predators as a pest. Shooting parties were organised to reduce numbers. The Lake District writer, Mary Armitt highlighted the situation. *"Then came the evil days and wholesale destruction of wildlife. A party of fox hunters working for the whole of Whit week in 1759, at the instigation of local farmers, shot in the Ullswater district alone 15 foxes, 7 badgers, 12 wild cats, 9 pine martens, beside a prodigious number of foumarts, eagles, ravens, kites, and other vermin."* There

Tales of a Lakeland Valley - BORROWDALE

is no reason to suppose that things were different in Borrowdale to Ullswater. However, eagles continued to survive in Borrowdale and William Gilpin recorded in his "Observations" written in 1772, based on a visit to the lakes in 1752, *"It is a common species of traffic in this country to supply the curious with young eagles; in which the inhabitants are very expert."*

William Gilpin also recorded an interesting anecdote that was related to him *"An eagle was seen at a distance, to pounce on its prey; which it carried, in a perpendicular ascent, aloft in the air; and hanging dubious for some time, it was at length observed to to descend in the same direct line; and it's fall, as it approached, seemed attended with an odd tumbling motion. It fell stone dead on the ground ; and a weasel, which it had carried up, and which had the address to kill its adversary in the air, being now at liberty, ran away."*

A more recent tale of the exploits of an escaping weasel was told by David Tyson who lives at Watendlath. "Ya day there was a crowd o' fellas talking at Rosthwaite and they got on aboot wizzles an' that. Somewhere in Johnny Wood theer's a wall, and some on them 'ad seen a wizzle gaa in that wall, so they rove wall doon to git at wizzle; but they nivver did git it. Bloody yards and yards of wall was rove doon and they nivver got wizzle yet."

Thomas West, father of Lake District guide book writers wrote his Guide to the Lakes in 1778, the eagle was still commonly seen in the Borrowdale valley, and remained a source of some considerable nuisance to its farmers. In his account, West described Borrowdale as a smaller and more confined valley than is generally regarded today.

"The most gigantic mountains that form the outline of this tremendous landscape, and inclose Borrowdale are, Eagle - Crag, Glaramara, Bull - Crag, and Sergeant - Crag. On the front of the first, the bird of Jove has his annual nest, which the dalesmen are careful to rob, but not without hazard to the assailant, who is let down from the summit of this dreadful rock, by a rope of twenty fathoms, or more, and who is obliged to defend himself from the attacks of the parent birds during his descent. The devastation made on the fold in the breeding season, by one eyrie, is computed at a lamb a day,..."

Eagle Crag lies a little way off the main road that runs through the Borrowdale valley. It can be easily found by turning down the narrow road that leads to Stonethwaite, from where a rough track leads to the junction of Langstrath and Greenup. Eagle Crag faces west, and its craggy ramparts once provided an ideal position for eagles to build their nest. Rocky ledges with sheltered overhangs were wide enough for a substantial nest of sticks to be built. Added to year by year, the untidy bulk contained a wool lined hollow cup, in which two eggs, warmed by the female's body, are incubated. Upstanding rock outcrops made for an ideal vantage point from which an "off duty" bird could scrutinise the ground for any likely prey; or provide a lazy perch on which to doze and digest a bloody gorging.

No eagle nests on Eagle Crag now, but why not sit beside the beck on a spring evening when the light lingers on the crag and allow your imagination to drift back in time. *The crag needs to be carefully studied for tell tale splashes of white droppings on the rock that gives the position of the nest site away. Stunted birch and rowan, that themselves have a hold of rock, partially cover the eagle's nest, but sit, and watch, and wait.*

Tales of a Lakeland Valley - BORROWDALE

A slight movement stirs the foliage as a tawny streaked head is raised above the nest; no sound, but piercing black eyes have detected a more distant movement still. A tiny speck at the valley head rapidly increases in size as broad wings sweep, then rise as extended legs search for a precarious hold on a trembling branch. The male brings in his prey to feed his mate.

Consider the size of the bird. The golden eagle is over thirty six inches from beak to tail; its broad, open tipped wings extend to a span of almost six feet. Its feet and talons are the size of a human adult hand; there is the strength of steel in their grip.

It is hardly surprising that the 18th and early 19th century valley folk were as concerned for the safety of their own children from the threat of eagle attack, as they were for their livestock. An account written by a reverend gentleman, Revd J C Atkinson, is of a tale told to him by Professor Wilson, a friend of William Wordsworth who recounted an attack by an eagle on a young child.

"...the infant was seized as it lay and slept where its mother had placed it, while herself busy not far off in the harvest field, and carried off by the strong bird to its eyry. The poor mother, frantic with her loss, blind to everything but the thought and effort for the recovery of her babe, safely scaled the precipice, high up on which the nest was placed; though no man however skilful and expert as a cragsman, had ever dared attempt the ascent; found her babe alive and unhurt and smiling in her face, descended again - a more perilous feat still - in safety, and once more on level ground at the foot, swooned helplessly away. The Eagles did not attack her in reality, though their fierce menaces made the spectators tremble." With the threat of this sort of happening, the Revd Atkinson saw it advisable to offer advice to lads when they went in search of eagle eggs. *"Our boy readers if ever they found an Eagle's nest might well need the protection of a good, strong cudgel, fearlessly and skilfully wielded, before they succeeded in possessing themselves of one of its eggs."*

Possession of an eagle egg in those early days was not merely to satisfy the kleptomaniac tendencies of an egg collector; for it provided additional means of supplementing the family income. A "bounty" could be claimed from the Crosthwaite Church wardens for the egg, young, or head of any adult eagle that was taken. This bounty also extended to the heads of ravens and foxes who were regarded as additional threats to the valley sheep. A rope was kept in the valley for the specific purpose of lowering a man down the crag to clear out an eagle's or a raven's nest for in the pre - rock climbing days, this was regarded as the only possible way to reach a crag.

One of the earliest bounty payments recorded in Crosthwaite Church records is in 1719, when Miles Wilson was paid one shilling for *"an old eagle."* In that same year, another eagle was taken by John Jackson on Armboth fell, which is part of the dividing range between Borrowdale and Thirlmere. This cost the Crosthwaite wardens another shilling. By contrast, some three years later, the going rate for the heads of young ravens was 2 pennies while an old bird was rewarded with a bounty of 4 pennies.

In 1731, Thomas Raven was paid one shilling by the church wardens for the heads of two young eagles, and inflation seemed to have had no effect on the economy, for 12 years later, a valley man by the name of Jonah Braithwaite was also paid 6d for ridding the valley of the menace of one young eagle.

Tales of a Lakeland Valley - BORROWDALE

The recovery of fox heads provided a more lucrative bounty for as long ago as 1722, the church wardens paid out 3/4 [about 17p] for an old fox and 2/- [10p] for a cub. It took John Wilson of Ashness the time and energy to recoup his 3/4 with a bag of one adult raven and five youngsters.

To ensure that the pack of dogs used for fox hunting were kept in a good order of obedience, the church wardens even paid Francis Hodgson 3d for a new lash for his dog whip. Eagles, foxes, ravens; none of them were any use as food items in their own right, yet they were hunted to the verge of extinction in England, to protect the flocks and livelihood of valley people. No doubt those hunters of long ago would consider the antics of today's bird watchers and "twitchers" with incredulity, for many travel great distances to catch a glimpse of a Lakeland golden eagle.

If it was possible for those valley folk of 200 years ago, to watch members of our environmentally aware generation reach for camera or binoculars to capture the flight of the golden eagle, they would no doubt be greatly distressed at the sight of 5 pence escaping from their guns, and their pockets.

The track from Stonethwaite leads to Eagle Crag at the junction of Greenup Ghyll and Langstrath

CHAPTER ELEVEN

Fell Running, Floods and Fatalities

Travel as far as you can into the Borrowdale valley and you will arrive at Seathwaite, pronounced locally as Sea'waite, which has earned the reputation of being "the wettest place in England." Anyone wanting to venture further into the hills must pass through Stan Edmondson's farm yard, which he described as "like a funnel on t' way to t' fells."

There must be few walkers who exchange a cheery "How're you doing?" greeting with Stan who are aware that he was one of the finest fell runners the valley has produced.

Stan's family came to the farm in 1916 and he grew up in Sea'waite where he has lived and farmed for almost all his life. "Ah was born to be a farmer", he says and as there was little else to do as a young lad spent most of his time helping on the farm, or "running wild on the fells."

Farm work came as second nature to Stan, not least the maintenance of miles of dry stone wall that a fell sheep farm demands. Stan Edmondson is extremely proud of the dry stone walls on his land of almost 3,000 acres that he rents from the National Trust. He repaired many of these walls himself and the stamina he built up, as a result of long days of walling or shepherding, stood him in good stead as a fell runner.

"Ah was allus slightly built, and very nimble. Ah was a bundle of energy when Ah was a kid, we were a wild bunch up here. When Ah used to go on t' fell to gather young lambs; we didn't need dogs, Ah just ran. Ah could catch a ewe without help of a dog. Ah was pretty fit then. After a spot of wallin' , Ah could mebbe be at bottom of t' fell before father and them got back home. There was no television in those days. You had to make your own entertainment. There was whist drives in the Institute, and the fellas would gather in the back bar of a pub. Women didn't go in there, they would have been looked down on. All the valley men were keen on fishing, most of them kept a trail hound and they liked to go hunting. Running was just something else to do." He recalled that all the quarrymen who lived in the valley kept beautiful gardens where they grew most of their own produce. "They were tough men them boys; real hardy Cumbrian men."

Stan's early competitive runs were in the Borrowdale Childrens' Sports, which he described as a "helluva day", when Ratcliffe's vans would come from Carlisle with baskets of ham filled buns. These were held in "whichever farmer's field happened to be right at the time." His first serious race was in 1946 when he entered the Guides Race at Grasmere Sports. He was taken there by Pont Pepper, a quarryman who lived at the Bowder Stone Cottage and is remembered by many folk for his collection of tethered birds of prey. These used to be viewed with interest by many visitors to the Bowder Stone.

Running at Grasmere gave Stan the first opportunity to run as a "professional", for prize money was paid to the winners. "Amateurs used to come to run, but they didn't give their real names. They weren't supposed to lift the prize money," he said. Although the prize money was not high, there was opportunity to make extra money by betting on the runners. Stan went to that Grasmere meeting confident in his own mind that he was good enough to win. but he was unsure of the proceedings. He didn't argue when told by "some fellas", that he was not expected to win. This didn't make sense to Stan who felt he could have "walked it", but he was new to the professional circuit, he did as he was told and came in fourth. "Ah think that would be the only time Ah did what Ah was told. Ah never did it again. Money didn't mean anything to me, it was the glory of winning."

By the time the following season of 1947 had come round, Stan had gained more experience and knowledge of what was expected of him, even to the extent of knowing that he would be far more successful if he wore the correct footwear. That realisation came in a race that he should have won quite easily. "Ah was runnin' in a pair of old soccer boots. Ah 'd a good lead goin' up, but comin' down m' feet felt like lead. Ah kept slippin' and tumblin' down. Ah come in second and collapsed over the line. A woman come forward an' give me a sip o' whisky. Ah was disgusted wi meself."

In those immediate post war years, the production of sports wear was not one of the country's major priorities as it struggled to regain an industrial footing. Running boots were virtually unobtainable. Stan went to see if former fell runner Bobby Gilpin of Portinscale had any running boots he no longer needed. "He was a great runner in his time, and he had some old uns that he said Ah could have. Ah wore them for t' next race at Rosthwaite. Laal Freddy Rayson was runnin', and he was good; he shot across t' field and I caught him near t' top of t' fell, and nivver saw him again. Ah turned at the top and came down, and Ah'll never fergit the shoutin' an' the hollerin' there was for t' local lad. Ah still hear it ringing in m' ears like."

The memory of that very first win has stayed clearly with Stan, but it certainly was not his last. The following Saturday he competed at Braithwaite and still wearing his borrowed boots he won that race. Two days later, it was the big one; Keswick Bank Holiday Sports, which Stan likened to Wembley, or even the Olympics as far as fell running was concerned. "It was the Mecca of Lake District sports. There was mebbe 12, or 13 thousand people or more." The course of the fell race was to the top of Latrigg and back. Stan described as being a difficult race because so much of it was run on hard road surface before the runners took to the fell. He won that race quite easily and went on from there to win many more.

The following year of 1948 was probably the peak of Stan's running career, for he won every race that he entered. "Ah was never beaten, Ah was so fit Ah felt as if Ah could almost fly. It felt like that anyway. Ah don't know what me mother fed us on, but it must have been good. It's a nice feelin' to be as fit as that."

Part of Stan's training was to do a three mile evening run on the flat land round the valley bottom. "Ah would do that before supper, Joe Cockbain would set me off, he was the trainer. It was like training Shergar! Ah came back, had me supper and then it was back to work again, clippin or haytimin'." Most of the fell races in which Stan competed were held on Saturdays, and that was his day off. A poached or scrambled egg formed his light breakfast before he set off for the race. "You get your butterflies and that before you set off, but once you start everything's alright."

Appendicitis curtailed Stan's fell running activities in 1949 and it took him a while to regain the standard of fitness that enabled him to compete again. 1950 wasn't a good year by his own high standards, but in 1951 when Bill Teasedale, the Caldbeck runner was at his height, Stan was fit enough to challenge him.

"Grasmere came on and Ah didn't think Ah 'd much of a chance, but the night before, Joe Cockbain and me went to have a look over it. At the top of the course, there's a crag. Well Ah allus came on the crag, but a lot o' the runners work their way round the back. Well anyways, Ah was sort of nimble in them days and Ah worked out a short cut up this crag. Ah rehearsed it once or twice and thought, if Ah 'm going to beat him, this is the way to do it."

As the runners set off and the race proceeded, it turned out as Stan anticipated. Bill Teasedale went round the back of the crag while Stan took his short cut which brought him to the summit almost the same time as Bill. "Ah'll never forget that look on his face, I went up my secret route, and came face to face with him at the flag. Ah don't think to this day he knows where I come from. He turned tail and Ah followed him round that second flag and right down that diagonal run. Ah was right at his heels. He crossed the gill at the bottom wood; he came to quite a high gate. Well, Bill tried to get up and he slipped right back. Ah put one, two hands on and vaulted gate, cos Ah could jump gates. Ah was a lot taller than Bill. The crowd, well they couldn't believe it; there was just a sigh went up. They were expectin' Bill to win. The whole crowd couldn't believe it like, that Ah'd won. And Bill 'I tell you himself, that was one of the best fell races there ever was. Bill was shattered, but mind he tried hard, and Ah did as well."

Although Bill Teasedale seemed unbeatable to many of those who followed the round of valley sports, records show that "Ah beat him more than he beat me, but he was a great little runner," said Stan.

There was one further occasion when Stan's enthusiasm to win was spurred by the suggestion that a race be fixed for someone else to take the top prize. Stan always entered races determined to win. As far as he was concerned, the prize money was immaterial, it was the thrill of winning that counted. As the starter's gun sent the field away, the anger and adrenalin surged within him. Stan flew ahead of the field and built up such a lead that it was impossible to break it down. "Ah 'd learned a bit by then. Ah flew that day" he said.

To the dismay of the "fixers", Stan won the race at bookies odds of 8 - 1. "All the locals had money on me that day, so they did alright out of it." he said.

Although Stan enjoyed his fell running days, he felt that after the tremendously successful year of 1948, he was never as fit again and much of the motivation had gone. "And anyway there was the job of running a 3,000 acre sheep farm to think about," he said.

Over the years, the reputation has grown that Seathwaite is "the wettest place in England" and although it may not rain more often than in other parts of the Lake District, when it does rain at Sea' waite it can be of such intensity as to cause severe devastation. "They reckon that Sprinkling Tarn area is where all this water falls. Now in one of my old sheep books, its printed as Printling Tarn, not Sprinkling Tarn." Stan said. The gathering rains that tumble down the natural fall of the land from the mountainous central core of the Lake District to the valleys below causes severe flooding. This occurs when the mass of water cannot escape sufficiently quickly. There are records of great floods in the eighteenth and nineteenth century. One in 1895 caused a tremendous amount of damage. Alan Mounsey of Grange recalled his father telling him of how they watched the river rising higher and higher just a short distance from the back of their house. "There's a needle of rock sticks up there and the water to rose to just three inches off the top. A little half drowned mouse crawled up and stayed there till the waters went down. He was very bedraggled, but he survived."

Two of the floods that occurred during Stan's lifetime remain very clear in his memory. In 1942 there was a flood that almost claimed the life of a visitor to Rosthwaite. There used to be wooden chalets that served as an annexe to the Scafell Hotel, and on the night of a tremendous storm, the heavy downpour of rain caused flooding to sweep through the chalets. While the inhabitants were attempting to reach the safety of the main hotel, a Mrs Forsyth was swept away. "It went with her, right down through the village; an' she caught on some barbed wire. If she hadn't o' caught on that barbed wire, she would ha' been drowned. Joe Bland, 'nd maybe one or two more got a rope and they went down. It was dark you know, but Joe went down on this rope and they found her, catched on this barbed wire in a bit of a hedge."

Stan maintains that if that particular flood had come at midnight, there would have been dozens of campers drowned. In his opinion, they were only saved because they were "washed out" before the main force of floods poured through the valley. Earlier in the day, a steady increase in the rain had prompted them to seek safety while it was still daylight. They sought shelter in barns and on higher ground, while many were taken into farms and hotels. Thus they escaped what could have been a very real tragedy.

"There was thunder and lightning and the rain was pouring down, just like sheets of water." The flood water funnelled through Stan's farmhouse, sweeping away the freshly delivered groceries and in the surrounding fields, it flattened the crop of oats that had been neatly stooked earlier that day. Stan recalled that above the roar of the wind, came an even louder noise, the sound of an explosion as an aircraft crashed further down the valley.

Jont Hind was a special constable in Borrowdale at the time and when the crash occurred he was directed to "go and see to it." The Borrowdale road was blocked by the severe flooding and this prevented the Keswick police getting into the valley. Willie Hind recalled his father's experience. "It was the worst job he ever had to do. The whole thing was burnt up. There was wreckage everywhere. They managed to get the bodies out, and then he had to stand a guard on it to stop folks from going with bits of it. They reckoned it was lost and it came through behind Castle and Gate Crag. If he hadn't hit Johnny Wood he was going to hit something."

At Seathwaite, the flood water level rose higher, and an ambulance that was waiting in the the farm yard to evacuate some injured climbers, was engulfed by the flood to such an extent that "the next morning its belly was to the ground with the gravel that had built up, and the shaves of oats was washed away to Keswick."

Stan has often seen the steady trickle of water that comes down Sour Milk Gill change to roaring torrent in less than an hour. This occurs during a severe thunderstorm and that was what happened in 1942. "There was a poor old camper camped down at bridge there on t' side of t' road. When he got back, his old tent and ivverything 'ed gone. Tent was still there, but it was hanging under t' bridge where it had caught. The ones that do the most damage are the sudden thunderstorms that bring like flash floods. It's on ye before you can do anything about it. And anyway, what could you do."

The worst flood that Stan can recall happened in 1966, when about six inches of rain fell in two or three hours. "It was one Saturday night and we went to t' Swinside pub, that was our haunt in them days. It was rainin' pretty heavy when we left about nineish." About an hour later, Stan received a phone call from his wife Nance to tell him that water was pouring through the farm. "There was nowt they could do, so they just oppened door and it went right through and out t' other side. There was bits o ' furniture going out wid it an' all; it was about three foot deep in t' house. They had to oppen t' door to let it out."

Fortunately the phone was intact, so Nance was able to keep assuring Stan that things were alright and as soon as possible he began to make his way back home. At Grange the river was so swollen that water was actually pouring over the top of Grange Bridge. "We couldn't git over Grange Bridge, all the wall tops was off at t' bridge; t' parapet walls was clean off." Obviously there was no way that Stan could reach home so he spent the night, waiting and watching, with one of his friends at what was then the post office. He recalled suddenly hearing a weird rushing sound that seemed to come up through the walls and after a while, the water started coming into that house. "It was about a foot deep in there. We were looking out o' t' bedroom window. We were terrified like." By early morning the rain had eased and the water started to go down. Stan was able to make his way back home, but not without difficulty. "John Bainbridge, he's dead now poor fella, he went in front of us clearing stones off t' road. You didn't know whether you were going to go into t' river or not, like. Anyway we got across and turned for home and got about to t' Bowder Stone and there was a car lodded in a tree across t' road; he was very lucky that fella."

The rest of the journey home was relatively uneventful, apart from a few minor floods at Rosthwaite , until he reached Seathwaite bridge. "And honestly it was a scene of devastation. Ah'd to leave vehicle there like, and walk rest o' t' way in fields. It was just trying to break daylight then an' Ah could see there was a car down t' field there." The car belonged to a couple, who in Stan's words, had gone down the quiet Seathwaite road for a bit of "cuddlin' ", but had been caught out by the flood. Stan talked to them later.

"T' lass sed, Are we not movin'? When they looked out, t' car was floatin down t' road, an' it stuck on t' wall end. Well they were that frightened, they kept gittin' out and gittin' stones to put in t' car to hod it down and after a bit it went wid it and int' t' field. Well they were stranded. It was unbelievable. The water was wall top height, it was like a big lake. The whole valley was completely flooded." Luckily, some members of K Shoes Mountaineering Club were staying in their Seathwaite Club Hut at the time, and they had rescued the couple from the car.

Stan's farm land was devastated by the flood. Walls were torn down at weaker spots through which water forced a way and thousands of tons of rocks and gravel was deposited on the fields, reminiscent of what it must have been like when the retreating glaciers of thousands of years ago left their scattered debris. For about a quarter of a mile from the farm, all the tarmac surface of the road was ripped up. "Comin' into t' yard, there was a hole there that you could have put a bus in; what a bloomin' mess."

Inside the farmhouse the floods had ruined everything; carpets, furniture, and books were all sodden. The flood water had gone, but it left behind its filthy mark. "The mud and the slime and the stench of it was awful. Anyway, we had to move upstairs and we were up there from September to the end of March. All the walls had to be chipped and replaced to about three foot. The stink was awful, you can't believe it."

In the farm buildings there was further devastation. The hay barn was flooded to a depth of three feet and much of that year's crop was destroyed. "People were marvellous," said Stan. "Keswick Mountain Rescue and anybody that would come and help. They moved the dry hay off the top of the wet so it didn't all waste. They helped to clear the fields of stones and that, all these volunteers were marvellous and we started to rebuild the walls on the lonnin's just a few days after."

Fortunately, as far as Stan was concerned, the loss to his livestock was relatively light. He lost about 30 sheep, but there was no loss of cattle. His brother however had fared much worse. "He lost all his hens and ducks. It wrecked all the sheds there. Even t' ducks was washed down to Keswick on to t' lake where they stayed and mated with the mallards." Stan reckons that the multi assortment of colours seen among the resident ducks on Derwentwater today, is due to the interbreeding with those that belonged to his brother, that were swept down by the floods.

To look at the neat, tidy walls and the trim farm buildings of Seathwaite today, it is hard to imagine that such a flood ever happened. "It was unbelievable because up to that time, we'd had such a great summer. Then the rain undid all that good. The weather men reckoned there was this great build up of clouds that just collapsed. Like a deck of cards I suppose."

One of the activities where Stan's fitness and knowledge of the Scafell and Great Gable ranges came in most useful, was in the developing field of mountain rescue, although he recalled that in his young days, there was no such organisation. "They'd just come down here and raise the alarm that there'd been an accident on Gable or wherever. Most of the quarry lads in Borrowdale were St. John Ambulance trained, so we'd get word up there They never stopped for anything to eat. They 'd mebbe worked all day , yet they they'd come up here on their push bikes to see what they could do and away they'd go. Anyways, they' d bring people down here, or maybe to Wasdale. Sometimes when they got down to Wasdale, they'd go to Wastwater Hotel and they wouldn't even give them a drink, even if it was a minute or two after time. And them poor lads had took whoever, dead or alive, all the way down there and then had to walk all the way back; and nivver a thing to eat since mebbe their sandwiches at bait time."

Stan feels most strongly that the quarrymen rescuers never had the recognition they deserved. "I don't think they wanted publicity, but real heroes they were, and that was in the thirties, long before mountain rescue started. There wasn't so many people walkin' on the fells, they were mainly climbing accidents then."

Stan had personal experience of being involved in rescues with some of those quarrymen that he regards as the real pioneers of mountain rescue. One such was a Borrowdale man, Bill Brown who was closely associated with St. John Ambulance in Keswick. He trained all the quarry lads in first aid, he organised courses and classes. "They were real hard men those quarrymen. Some of them, the single men would go to Keswick and blow all their money on drink, and then come back to the stone huts where they lived at quarries."

Seathwaite Farm was inevitably one of the first places to which an accident was reported and was also used as a temporary mortuary. Stan recalled that one night a young couple who had been killed in a climbing accident on Great Gable, were brought to his barn. On the same night, the tally of bodies rose with the addition of a woman who was killed in an accident in Grains Gill. "That was three of them lying there in just one night" he said. "What happened in them days, they left them in the barn over night; not only them, but many, many others besides and Young's haulage wagon used to come next day and tek them to t' mortuary in Keswick. That's the way it worked. Even if t' ambulance come, and the person died a hundred yards from this door, they would just drive away. They would never take a dead body. They would leave them in our barn to be collected next day in the haulage wagon."

When news of an accident reached Seathwaite Farm, Stan had no hesitation in responding and enlisting the help of quarrymen to join in the rescue. "There was a lecturer, a professor from Jesus College, an' his wife fell and broke her leg on Gable face, nearest Windy Gap. Word came down here that it was badly broke, so Ah went to Seatoller and got a van, or summat, and they'd an old Thomas stretcher. Anyways there was Cockbain twins, there was Bill Jackson, Nancy's brother; they were only young uns; they were hardly in their teens, and there was Cecil Howard. There was about five of us. We got to t' top of Honister and we walked up Drum House up to Windy Gap and we got her on the stretcher like. There was only them two there. We got her down and it was hard work with that stretcher. They were only young lads like that was carryin' ; I was mebbe only 21. It was quite a long haul and night was cutting in. We got away along Moses Trod and we finally got to t' Drum House. Well, it's darker when you're coming down into t' valley, an' the light was gone. We even had to stop to strike matches just to see where we were at. We got down to t' top of Honister and here was Jim Egglestone and Keswick ambulance."

Some Keswick mountaineers had also responded to give assistance, but they took a different route to that taken by Stan and his helpers. "You see Ah've been born here and run about here all my life. Ah know all the nooks and crannies. Well, we completely missed them. We didn't even know they were coming."

A formal Mountain Rescue Team was formed in Keswick in 1946, under the leadership of Colonel Rusty Westmorland and Stan joined it in 1947. His local knowledge of the area proved invaluable in many rescues, for not only could he guide the Team to the scenes of incidents, but he was also familiar with grass descents down which the stretcher could be lowered much more quickly and easily than effecting "a carry" over rough ground. Stan was a member of the team for over thirty years, but was mostly involved in rescues within the vicinity of his farm. He reflected that the composition of the rescue teams has changed greatly over the years as they have, of necessity, taken on a much more professional approach. "At one time they were all local lads," he said.

Mountain rescue was not a new activity in the Borrowdale valley for on 22 June 1878, an account appeared in the local paper, The West Cumberland Times. *"On Wednesday last, Keswick was startled from its tranquillity by a report that yet another visitor had been lost on the mountains, and a search party included Messrs. H I Jenkinson, T Mayson and D. Lancaster was organised to go on a voyage of discovery for the missing man. It appears that on the previous day a clergyman was on the Buttermere coach as far as Seatoller and proceeded on foot to Scafell, the summit of which he scaled. He was armed*

Tales of a Lakeland Valley - BORROWDALE

with a Jenkinson Guide, and seems not to have sufficiently consulted his mentor, for on return he took the left, instead of the right hand path which brought him in due course to Langdale. ... He considered discretion the better part of valour and resolving to have no more adventures that night, remained in the snug hostelry. Meanwhile, when he did not turn up in Keswick on Wednesday morning, much alarm was felt, and the search party above named were within five minutes of starting when a telegram arrived from Grasmere in the nick of time."

Another rescue that is fixed in Stan Edmondson's memory took place on what started out as a beautiful March day." There was a party set off from Derwent Bank Holiday Fellowship place. They went up Corridor route on Scafell Pike and they got on top. They started to come down and this girl slipped. She'd come down in a col, so they went round and shouted. I think they were too petrified to gaa an' look for her. Anyways, it was still quite a nice day, though t' wind was blowin' up a bit, so we went up there and found her aback of the big stones. She'd been dead awhile. All her clothes and her back were worn away, she wouldn't stand a chance 'cos its all rock in theer. It come on a real blizzard and we went down Brown Tongue to the Fell and Rock climbing hut that I'd never been in before. We stopped there, for what a hell of a blizzard it was. It would mebbe be four or five o ' clock before Keswick lot came round for us. Eh, it was a long night that."

The alarm was raised at Seathwaite once at five o clock in the morning, which interrupted Stan's sister at some early morning baking. "A fella came to the door in a terrible state, RAF man he was. They'd crashed up in t' fells somewhere, but he didn't know where he'd come down. The mist was down and he didn't just know where they'd come down. Anyways, they got Borro'dle school headmaster, Mr Boustead, and they'd gathered anybody they could get."

The only hard information that the rescuers were given was that the airman had come down by a waterfall. They came to the conclusion that this was Taylorgill Force and so made their way up beside the fall. Finding nothing there, they carried on to Green Gable from where Watson Boustead "gave this big scream out, he'd found it. Pilot was still sitting in his seat, what a mess his face was! We got him on a stretcher, but he died coming down. I think there was two survived , but t' rest were killed."

There was another occasion when Stan was going to Ennerdale on a murky sort of morning to gather sheep from the fells that overlook that valley. He dropped down towards the Black Sail hostel and looking back into the rocky morraine below Windy Gap that separates Green Gable from Great Gable, he saw what he could only describe as "this yellow stuff". He was used to seeing the visitors to the CHA hostel at Seatoller going out in bad weather wrapped in yellow capes. His first reaction was that it was a party of hostellers who had gathered together for a meal break. As he dropped down towards the Black Sail hut, he saw a pony and trap being driven, "hell for leather" up the rough road. "Ah got down to t' hostel and there was two airmen in there. They'd kicked the door in and they weren't sae bad. " Stan went to investigate the "yellow stuff", which turned out to be the fuselage of an aeroplane. No one else had survived the crash, apart from those who had made their way to Black Sail hut.

One of the worst crashes that Stan recalls occurred in the Borrowdale valley when a bomber crashed into Johnny Wood. in 1942. "I've never seen such carnage, there was eight or nine on board. I think it was a Wellington and they were all Canadian crew. It was terrible; it was just like a tin heap. The biggest part of it was the engine. The rest was just bits o' tin. There's no doubt it had a load o' bombs on like. And it burned trees and all around.''

That was a night of tragedy indeed, for the plane crash in Johnny Wood occurred on the same night as the fatal accident on Great Gable, and the same night as the flood. Philosophically Stan Edmondson observed that while many rescues turned out all right, others inevitably ended in tragedy.

Members of Keswick Mountain Rescue Team refine their techniques with regular practises. A volunteer provides the "casualty" on this occasion. Often it's the real thing!

*Stan Edmondson, 2nd right with hand on knee, awaits the gun
to start the fell race.*

The aftermath of the flood at Seathwaite Farm.

CHAPTER TWELVE

Some Minor disasters

Aeroplane crashes, and mountain accidents are serious incidents that inevitable cause heartache and grief. Over the years, however there have been many minor incidents in Borrowdale which may have been serious at the time, but now provoke laughter when recalled. One such incident occurred on the Watendlath Road when a farmer from the hamlet was returning from Keswick market one Saturday.

"There was this farmer that 'ed bin to t' market in Keswick. He went in his light trap, but he had a lot o ' drink and he was ower the worse for it. It's a good job his hoss knew t' way home 'cos t' farmer fell asleep. He gits to t' Watendlath road as far as t' Barra yat. Weel, he was weel away. T' horse stopped at gate, an 'some on t' lads saw it. They unyoked the horse and took it through t' gate. When they got to t' other side, they closed t' gate and yoked hoss through it. They left t' old farmer theer sleeping it off. What a helluva row there was when he woke up and f'und out what they'd done."

Watendlath was the scene of another incident involving some goats. When William Gilpin made his journey through the area in 1752, he observed that the rocky nature of the ground at Watendlath would be ideal for goats as they could graze the vegetation that was inaccessible to other animals. Some goats did arrive at Watendlath, but it was not as a result of Gilpin's observations.

"Jerry had some hoggs away for t' winter. Well they'd done rather badly, so to compensate him for them, t' fella give him these two or three goats. There was a great white billy amang them. Grace, Jerry's wife, was ligging abed when they come. Her bedroom backed on to t' fell. T' old white billy come and looked in t' skylight. It was a moonlight night. They said it near flait her to death, but then the' say she was a rather nervous body."

David Tyson recalled that when he was a lad at Watendlath there was "quite a swarm of goats", and told of how Johnny Richardson, former hunstman with the Blencathra, and his own brother, John Tyson earned themselves each a sixpence. " Owld Hunty and our John was coming frae skeul and they heard these shouts and screams and yells for help. There was this woman said that t' old billy goat had tackled her, but what really happened they never knew. She'd got hold of it b' t' horns, but didn't know what she was ganna deow next. They got it away from her and took it aback o ' holly tree and give it a bloody good hiding. Ah dunno what good that would deow like. Next morning at skeul, t' maister asked for the two gentleman that had rescued the lady, to stand up. He had two envelopes and there was a sixpence in each, and that was a lot of money then."

Dick Richardson told another tale concerning hoggs. "There used to be a fella did a bit o' work up here for Billy Wilson. They called him Jummy Dover, he was killed in t' quarries in 1925. Old Billy used to put his crab hoggs out in t' turnip field . Well Jimmy used to like to come up here for a bit o' shootin', and' he come up this night to shoot hares. Anyway, he come wid his gun to t' turnip field and he shot Billy's hoggs by mistek' ; he thowt they were hares!!!"

Tales are told about Ben Pattinson, the Longthwaite farmer who managed to get everywhere even with the handicap of his wooden leg. His daughter Peggy Horsley recalled the time that her father tried to get a new clog. "He wanted a clog for his good leg. Will ye git me a clog at Dalzell 's, he asked his mate. Well, betime George got to Keswick, he couldn't remember which leg dad wanted t' clog for, so he went outside to think. Just then, Pont Pepper was gaan past.

Which wooden leg is Baps? said George.

Pont couldn't think for a minute, Oh hell, Ah don't know, he said.

They stood away for a bit, then Pont said, Which leg does he put out when he's playing darts."

With that reminder to help them, Bap was provided with a new clog for his left foot!

Firing chimneys with bracken at spring cleaning time was often the cause of house fires. "Our old lass had a trick when spring cleaning o' gaan to t' barn for an armful of brackens an' push them up t' chimney an' set them leet. Ah've seen us down t' bottom there an' seen smoke and thowt ay she's cleanin' oot t' chimney, but many a time she'd set t' beams afire in t' house."

Dick Richardson was working at the Borrowdale saw mill when the fire engine went hurtling down the valley with lights flashing and klaxon blaring in its attempt to get a clear run down the narrow road. "Somebody sez to me, They've set fire to your house. Ah sez, Ney be buggered! Wouldn't it be a bugger if they had - and God damn it, it was..."

Two elderly residents in Rosthwaite were sitting by their fire one dark winter's night, where the only lighting in the room came from candles. Suddenly, the room was plunged into darkness. "Some on the lads were devils in those days. Two o' them had climbed up on t' roof and they popped a chicken down t' chimney. When it got to t' bottom, wid a' t' flutterin' and squawkin' it put t' candles out. T' chicken was gaan roond and roond t' room and there was sek a lot o' stir. T' old folk run out wid their blankets roond them; they didn't know what was gaan on."

Before the advent of electricity and the luxury of sophisticated plumbing facilities, the farms and cottages of Borrowdale had none of the modern comforts that we take for granted today. Even as late as the 1920's and 30's, earth closets were still in use and these consisted of nothing more than a stone building that contained a pit in the floor, over which was a boarded seat with a hole in the middle. Some households had a double seated facility! "You just threw a shovel of earth over it, and a bit later it would be cleaned out an mebbe spread on t' field." recalled one former user.

To save a dash across the yard on a cold, wet night, the use of chamber pots in bedrooms was accepted as quite normal, even in some of the hotels. It was the use of of a chamber pot in a farmhouse that led to an embarrassing experience for one Watendlath man who was home on leave during the second world war. "It would be 1941- 42, the year of the bad snow blow when we had to tunnel our way out of the house" said David Tyson. "The tarn was frozen over and ivverything was frozen up. This fella had to use chamber pot upstairs. He fetched it down to throw it outside. I can see him yet; big coat on, soldiers hat on t' side o' t' head. He went out o' t' door and instead o' throwing wid wind, he threw it agin t' wind. I can see him noo; he was absolutely covered; he daren't open his mouth to speak, he just come spluttering away."

A related family to Dick Richardson lived at Stepps End Farm before David Tyson took it over. One member of that family was Dick's cousin Joss. David remembered a tale about Joss going to have a bath. " One night Old Jerry was sitting ya side o' t fire reading paper, and Grace was at t' other. Well, great Joss, and you know what a size he was , he went for a bath. Well, he filled bloody bath up to t'rim an' got in. 'N all this water come running through the ceiling and they just sat theer fer lang enough watchin' water drippin' doon afore they fun out what it was."

Joss seemed to have an affinity for disaster involving water, for on another occasion, he tried an experiment to see how far he could walk with his eyes shut. "There was a laal plank bridge ower t' beck" said David, " an' he tried to walk across wid his eyes shut. Well, he walked off bloody edge didn't he. He went up yam into t' back kitchen door, an' he was stannin' a back o' t'door twining towel up . He was wet through do you see. His mother, Grace come. What's wrong Josey, she asked him. I tumbled off t' bridge. Wanted to see hoo far a' could walk wid my eyes shut."

As you leave the hamlet of Stonethwaite, a rough track leads to the junction of the Greenup and Langstrath paths. Turn right through the gate and enter Langstrath. A little way beyond are the tumble-down remains of a dwelling house. The walls still stand, but only just; while the roof has long since fallen down. A few timbers still lie there among the nettle beds. The house is marked on the Ordnance Survey map as Johnny's House and is of considerable age, for as long ago as 1870, it was recorded as being a ruin. Willie Hind, who lives in Stonethwaite has a theory that the house was once used as a summer home for a herdsman who moved cattle into the valley for summer pasture. "We allus remember it as Jwohn hoos, and Jwohn hoos yat, an' Jwohn hoos brig in that spot." said Willie.

The building may well have taken the name of such a character, but in view of the lack of documentation, the matter is open to speculation. A tale has been handed down over the years that has become part of Cumbrian folklore, but whether it is fact or fiction is for the reader to decide. It concerns a trick played on Jwohnny and his wife by two Langdale men who walked over the Stake on their way to Keswick.

Jwohnny's house was handily situated on the route to supply the passing traveller with a bite of haver bread and cheese and a jug of ale, for although it was not an inn, the inhabitants followed the traditions of offering Cumbrian hospitality to satisfy the needs of travellers. It was of necessity simple fare, for the couple depended on their own resources of their few animals, crops, and store of oatmeal, in much the same way as other valley folk. They enjoyed a crack with passing travellers, for their only regular company came with their Sunday visit to church, or their weekly journey to the market in Keswick, where they sold besoms. They made these "witches broomsticks" from materials they gathered on the fell.

One Friday night Jwohnny and his wife went to bed early in readiness for the next day's long walk to market. So deeply did they sleep that they failed to be roused by two men who had travelled over from Langdale. As the lads were unable to get a reply to their knocking, they decided to play a trick on the old couple. They gathered arms full of bracken from Jwohnny's bracken stack, and stuffed every window and crack where a chink of light would penetrate into the house. Then they carried on to Keswick, where after a rough night's sleep they had a roisterous day spent in the town's many inns and taverns . The market was all hustle and bustle, but of Jwohnny and his wife there was no sign. At the end of the day, the two lads managed to stagger their way back down the valley. It was dark when they came to Jwohnny's house, where there was still no sign of life. Staggering and chortling from a combination of high spirits and their over indulgence, they hauled the brackens away from the windows and doorway and put them back on Jwohnny's stack stack, before carrying on their way back to Langdale.

When Jwohnny eventually stirred to the onset of daylight next morning, he woke up his wife and urged her to get ready to go to market. They gathered their besoms together and heavily loaded set off for Keswick.

When they reached Rosthwaite, they could hardly believe their eye; people were dressed up in their Sunday best clothes. This was too much for a confused Jwohnny who couldn't understand why folks were going to church on a Saturday.

"It's Sunday, man" said one to Jwohnny.

"We've laid in bed, theer's nowt sa sure, ower two neets an' a day", Jwohnny was forced to reply with great embarrassment, as he sheepishly made his way back home.

Occasionally visitors to Borrowdale valley become totally lost, and wonder how they can make their way back on to the major road network. Personal encounters with such motorists include a couple who ended up on Honister Pass. They wanted to know if they were on the right road for Blackpool! Some problems occur because of either faulty maps, or faulty map reading skills. The hamlet of Stonethwaite is now at the end of a metalled road; it is a dead end as far as most motor vehicles are concerned, but rough tracks do lead away to cross over the fells to reach other valleys. Willie Hind told the tale of a motorist who landed in trouble through problems with his map

"Way before the war in the twenties sometime, there was a fella called Archie Connor ploughing that field below the bridge. It was a tatie field at that time. He was ploughing away one morning, and this fella comes in a car and stops on t' bridge and shouted across til him.

Can you tell me if I'm on the road to Grasmere?

Aye , he ses, well you are in a way, but you can't git with that thing.

Oh yes, I've got a map here which shows there's a good road all the way from here. Do I turn right through this ghyll?

Aye that's right, turn that way, if that's what it sez on your map. Away you go."

The direction the insistent motorist took was along a narrow rough track that climbs between dry stone walls and ultimately leads to Greenup Ghyll and over the fells to Grasmere.

Willie took up the tale again; " Well he got about a hundred yards on and he got stuck atween two gurt steans, and he could git ney farther. Anyway, he got fast, an' he come back an' he shouted to Archie, I've got stuck, could you unhitch your horse and pull me out.

Archie said, When Ah've finished plooin' this field Ah will, but Ah'll be a bit.

Well, fella was gitten madder be t' time.

Archie said, Ah warned ye afoor ye set off ye wadn't git far wid that thing.

He said, Ah plood away til it was gittin' dark and then Ah went and pulled him out. Ah said it'll mebbe larn 'im next time to tek notice o' t' locals."

For some years, Willie Hind worked in the Information Centre at the foot of Honister Pass and there he had experience of walkers getting into difficulties with their planned routes.

"Some people go on to the fells on bad days, and you warn them against it , but they won't take any notice; they've come a long way and they' ll say, We're going.

One come in one day, and it was snowing, well half snowing; it was just about Easter time. He said, I've come to leave you my route. I'm going over Green Gable to Great Gable. I'm dropping down to Beck Head and into Wasdale, then I'm going to come back over Scafell Pike and down Allen Crags and back down to you. I'll stay overnight at

Wasdale."

Willie said, "Well its nice of you to tell us where we'll be able to look for t' body. You won't get far. There's a blizzard on Green Gable. You'll never get to Great Gable today."

The walker had driven up over 200 miles from the Midlands and was determined to make the most of his weekend.

"Well now then, you can't say I didn't warn you" said Willie, as the walker set off ignoring his advice. "Well there was nowt Ah could do. It was no use tellin' Mountain Rescue; they didn't want rescue as far as Ah knew. Anyway, he landed back in afore Ah closed about half past four in t' afternoon. He was just about done in; he was blue." I've just come in to apologise, he was good enough to say. And away he went back home.

Track into Langstrath with the remains of Johnny House

CHAPTER THIRTEEN

A Quarryman's Tale

Motorists, cyclists and walkers who make their way up Honister Pass as it rises out of Borrowdale to form the main route into the neighbouring valley of Buttermere, may wonder at the debris of slate that cascades down the fell sides. But behind the grey forbidding sides of the fells, there is a story of a traditional Lake District industry that was carried on for almost 400 years. Some authorities claim that the Honister green slate was used as far back as Roman times. Usage in local buildings probably dates to the seventeenth century as is indicated on the date stones of some valley dwellings.

Earliest form of transporting the slate away from the area would probably have been by pack horse. The port of Ravenglass would be the most likely to be used for exporting the slate from Cumberland, as there is a direct pack horse route from Honister into Wasdale and thence to the coast. Legend has it that a Moses Rigg was a quarryman and smuggler, who used his string of pack ponies for carrying slate in one direction, and smuggled spirits across the fells in the other. The path, or sledgate that he followed is still known as Moses Trod and crosses the head of Ennerdale and into Wasdale. Moses was also reputed to have illicit stills hidden away among the quarry workings where he made his own fiery brand of spirits.

The slate was extracted either by open quarrying or tunnelling. Much further down the fell, and of easy access from Honister Hause is the Kimberley vein. A mine road leads to the now disused workings where two stone buildings still remain. These comprise a generator house and a cabin for the workmen. The breeze block construction is incongruous against the background of slate where they stand out like the proverbial, "sore thumb". In this former industrial landscape, the old huts of early slate construction, harmonise with their surroundings and make no intrusion. Rather they create a source of wonder that the old time workers could not only extract the slate, but they had the skills to build long lasting, and weatherproof shelters. One was high on Honister Crag at the Ashgill outcrop quarry; two were at Dubbs, another was near Bull Ghyll gorge. There were three huts near the Hause, and one near the outcrop workings of Yew Crags. There was also a sledgers' hut alongside the road to Buttermere. Later more accommodation was needed for the quarry workers and between 1893 and 1918 the company built a number of houses in and around Seatoller.

In the quarry workings, the blocks of slate were blasted away from the quarry walls with the use of gunpowder. This was inserted into hand drilled holes that had been made with the use of sharply pointed metal rods driven with a hammer, "It could tek up to a week to drive in one o' these holes. You can allus tell a hand driven hole, it's sort o' three sided."

A heavy hammer called a tulley, and a wedge shaped tool called a set, were used for splitting the blocks of slate along the cleavage planes. The tulley was later replaced with

77

a heavy wooden mallet with four iron bands. It weighed about 21 lbs. For splitting slates to their finished thickness, a small mallet, about one and a half pound in weight and a chisel 9" long with a point two and half inches wide and half an inch thick were used.

In later years, the use of electric drills and diamond saws made the work much easier, but the dressing and trimming tools remain much the same in quarries that are still working today.

Richard Brownrigg, of Keswick, spent 58 years of his working life at the quarries. He left Borrowdale school at the age of 14, and two days later began work as an apprentice at Honister Quarries. There was little choice of employment for the Borrowdale lads; it was farming or the quarries for school leavers in 1928. As three former generations of the Brownrigg family had opted for the quarries, it was almost inevitable that Richard should follow.

He recalled the first day that he started work. It was New Year's Day 1928, "There was no Bank Holiday then." Dick recalled that he felt a bit strange on that cold January day, for he was just a lad among a lot of men, even though many were familiar to him. "There was no How do Jack when you talked to them in those days. It was Mister this and Mister that."

Dick had to make a choice from the three trades that were available. There was the rockhand,(who actually mined the slate and worked underground); a river, (who split the slate), or a dresser,(who trimmed the slate to its finished state). Dick opted to be a river. Which ever trade he had chosen involved a five year apprenticeship where the young lad worked alongside a skilled man as part of a "bargain".

The "bargain" was, in effect, a team of workers. It could be as many as half a dozen, for the number in the "bargain" depended on the amount of work that had to be done. That was usually the production of finished and dressed slate, but other jobs indicated in the "Bargain Letting" book of 1927/8 involved widening, clearing rubbish at 4d a ton, and arching. The "bargain" would negotiate a price for a particular job which had to be completed over a specified period, and a contract would be signed by management and men. The cost of candles, fuses and explosives was deducted from the agreed price before the money earned was shared out. Dick likened the different levels of workings to a series of shelves, with each bargain working a particular shelf, or a part of that shelf.

At the end of the five year apprenticeship, "If you were any good, you could transfer to any bargain." But during that five years, working life at the quarry was hard and dangerous. There was no daily transport to take the men from the valley to their work place. Dick, like many of the quarrymen walked to his work place which was 1,000 feet up to the top of Honister Pass, from his Seatoller home. His working week lasted for five and a half days, and he worked from 7.30am to 5pm on weekdays, and finish at 12.30 on Saturdays. "If you didn't go to work on Saturday, you didn't get paid." He recalled that he was paid half a crown a day during the period of his apprenticeship.

The green slate of Honister Quarries was then in great demand to be used as building and roofing material. Although much of the quarrying was done to order, there was always a ready supply available for instant collection. The quarried and dressed slate was brought down to the Hause from the fellside workings on old sledges. Records exist that show 16 or 17 trips a day were completed in the early 19th C, with approximately a quarter of a ton of slate taken on each trip. One former sled run, that later had a "drum track" for hauling and lowering tubs of slate from Dubs Quarry, is now a popular walking path.

As the demand for slate grew, the original method of transportation by pack horses became an impossibility. They were superseded by horse drawn carts along what is referred to as the "new road" that was constructed for their own transport purposes by the quarry owners. It can still be followed as it curves away from the tar macadam surfaced road that still tests vehicles and drivers with its 25% gradients. This road was unsurfaced before 1935 and provided a test of nerve for visitors making the coach journey from Keswick by way of Honister and Newlands. Beatrix Potter recommended the same journey "as a cure for the colic".

Transport costs were built into the price of the slate and a document of 1884 records the following delivery charges.

sleighing from the workings to the incline top 1/8

Unloading the wagons and taking back the empties horse and man .... -/9

Horse hire from the incline foot to the loading stage for carts and machine .... -/7

Carting to the railway (Keswick) 9/-

Loading onto trucks .... -/6

By the time that Dick started to work at the quarries, there were lorries to collect the slate to take it to Keswick Railway Station. The lads were taken off their own jobs to see to the loading. This was done under the watchful eye of the check weighman. "I've seen as many as seven lorries waiting to be loaded when we got to work, and I've loaded 40 tons of slate before 10 o'clock". He recalled that it didn't matter what the weather was like, hail, rain, sleet or snow, "That was one of the apprentices' jobs; we had to run out the slate to stack it on the wharf (raised bank) where we loaded it on to the lorries."

Quarrying was not the only occupation at Honister, for to sustain the economic production of slate, joiners, blacksmiths, dressers, brakemen, wallers, loaders, carters, labourers as well as apprentices were all needed. The main accommodation for miners who lived too far away to walk to work every day, was in a hostel on the summit of the Hause. Another former quarryman, the late Dick Jackson who lived at Mountain View in Borrowdale recalled some of the conditions there. "They were cold, damp, dark places. There was no, what you would call, decent lighting or heating. It was so dark that one old fella nearly eat a cockroach that was on his bread and jam. Cold hands, cold feet and trying to keep warm is what I remember about t' quarries."

The original miners barracks that was used from 1927, was transferred to the YHA during the period of the second world war, when the quarries were closed down, and most of the machinery removed. The present youth hostel replaced the earlier one and was constructed in 1962 by John Holmes junr, of Elterwater.

After successfully completing his apprenticeship as a river, Dick became check weighman at the quarry in 1938. This job included being in charge of the issue of tallow candles, fuses, and carbide, organising repairs of tools and seeing the "bargains" were paid, as well as overseeing the weighing of the slate before it left the quarry. "We used to weigh four lots of five and a half hundredweight ; that meant twenty two hundred-weight to the ton because we used to allow two hundredweight for breakages."

An old counterfoil book of the Westmorland Green Slate Company shows that slate went all over the country.

4tons 4cwt, to Accrington High School;

14tons 14cwt to Almondbury Grammar School, Huddersfield;

5 tons St. John's College York, to name only three destinations.

Injuries to the work force at the quarries were quite frequent as an old Accident Book records. Some of its fragile pages still show bloodstains from accidents that occurred over fifty years ago. It is immediately obvious that hand injuries were the most common.

"Champed finger of left hand"; "lacerated palm"; "severed tendon" outnumber records such as "foreign body in sight".

It was a difficult task to get speedy treatment for an injury that occurred at work. There was an ambulance man, but most treatment for even serious injuries was administered by the workmates who did what they could. Dick explained that serious injuries were treated by the company doctor and an ambulance was brought to the quarry to transfer the injured workman to hospital, which was usually at Keswick. Although there was no protection afforded by safety clothing, a number of the head injuries were incurred through the men not taking correct safety precautions. "If the safety catch was not put on the hand winch, the handle could fly up and hit a man on the head." Dick explained. Evidence of this is found in the entries in the Accident Book which records such examples.

"Caught on head with crab handle (crab winch), causing cut over eye"

"Caught on mouth with crab handle when lifting a block. Bruised mouth."

The nearest hospital was at Keswick, and when Dick bought a new car in 1935, he found that within the first twelve months it was used 18 times to take injured quarrymen to hospital for treatment. On one occasion, he declined to travel alone in his car with a man who had a very severe head injury. The ambulance man had rendered first aid by pouring half a bottle of iodine into the open wound. "I didn't want to be alone with him; I thought he might go wrong in the head" was Dick's reaction.

One record of an accident had a special significance for Dick. It concerned Reuben Dover, of Dove Cottage, Stonethwaite who was his uncle. The Accident Book record for October 5th 1925 reads as follows.

Reuben Dover. Oct 2nd 9.45 morning..Far Rd End Quarry...

"When preparing for dressing in, a piece of rock fell whilst in ladder, breaking same and causing severe injuries. Torn Thigh, femur injured, Scalp wounds, back & abdominal injuries. Proved fatal on Oct.3rd at Carlisle Infirmary."

The original entry on the day of the accident reads, "Whilst dressing in & examining forebreast, a piece of rock fell, breaking the ladder and causing Dover to fall on floor. Lacerated thigh, muscle, bone, Bruises to back, head & Arm. Proved fatal on October 3rd at Carlisle Infirmary, from shock.

Dick explained that an area did not become known as a quarry until it was opened out from the initial 6 feet x 6 feet tunnel. Some of the workings were expanded into caverns thirty or forty feet in height and it was more comfortable inside these workings during the winter time, than on the open windswept crags of Honister. Snow and ice, and especially a certain wind that swept up the Buttermere valley, and was known as The Crack", created uncomfortable working conditions. That wind came in such vicious gusts that it was known to hurl a man off a crag and even lift a roof from a building, "I've known us laid off for weeks because there was no water to cool the saws. In 1935 we were off for six weeks because of heavy snow."

Diamond tipped circular saws that were used in the quarries to cut the slate into workable sized pieces had replaced the traditional method of breaking the blocks, which was called docking up. Although these saws made the job easier, they had to be constantly cooled by running water. Frozen water pipes could be thawed in the warmer temperature that occurred at the face workings deep inside Honister Crag, but this was often at the expense of hands that became frozen to the pipes. Frozen becks were another matter, for without the constant stream of water to cool saw blades, no cutting could be done. "We had to wait for nature to take its course." Even the cold itself was a hazard. Dick recalled how on one frosty morning, an engineer passed out with the cold and collapsed. "I took to carrying a small flagon of whisky in my waistcoat pocket after that; just in case it happened again."

Dick remembers the time when, what is now, the main road over Honister was unsurfaced. To make for easier transportation of slate away from the quarry, the Westmorland Green Slate Company constructed their own road. It was maintained by the quarrymen who regularly dressed the surface with a covering of slate chippings and waste. The gradients on the quarry road are quite gradual, and if other vehicles, not on quarry business wished to use it, a toll had to be paid. This was collected at the foot of the pass by a Mrs Bird who lived in one of the Seatoller cottages. Two of the earliest vehicles to work on Honister were a traction engine and a steam lorry. Kenneth Robinson, of Troutdale explained that there is still a part of Honister Pass that is known as Traccy Stand. "That's where the traction engine used to pause to get breath; right at the steep bit. It's a bit wider there, and it used to pull off the road to get steam up. I remember the Foden, the steam lorry; I used to run out of the house whenever it came down the valley." The steam lorry, which was named The Mountaineer, used to carry slate to Keswick railway station. "They took slates all over the place" said Kenneth, whose father worked at the quarry. "My father was very proud because some of them went to Central Hall, Westminster." The quarry road, is still known locally as "the new road", while the steeper and more direct tar macadamed road is called "the old road".

Dick Brownrigg went on to became manager of the Honister Quarries, from where he retired in 1985. "I've never done an hours work for anybody else" he said. One of the highlights of his career came in 1966 when the Duke of Edinburgh, along with a number of civic dignitaries visited the quarries and it was Dick's responsibility to give the Duke a guided tour." He said he would come back; but he never did."

The quarries at Honister are closed now. The workings are empty, providing shelter for sheep or foxes. Bilberry, heather and ferns grow over banks of slate that tumbles down the fell sides. The bridge across the road that once carried a tramway from Yew Crags to the diamond saws of the cutting shed, is long since gone. "I helped to put that bridge up in the 1930's," Dick recalled. The quarry yards are still littered with huge blocks of slates, the riving and dressing sheds are boarded up, and rusty circular saw blades lie

Tales of a Lakeland Valley - BORROWDALE

abandoned.

But, there is still, in Dick's opinion plenty of top quality slate that could be quarried. "But it won't be taken out like we used to take it. The quarrymen have gone, and their skills have gone with them; anyway, I don't think the young uns of today would put up with the work that we had to do."

Another former quarryman is Tommy Richardson, who lives in Keswick, and he found a complete contrast in the harsh, cold conditions at the quarry to his former job at the Low Briery Bobbin Mill. When the bobbin mill closed in 1959, Tommy had worked there for 34 years, but the next 24 brought not only a change of scene, but a change of climate; "I managed to get a job in slate quarry carry on, it was cold on top of Honister, hell it was cold; it was a big change for me, 'cos inside at bobbin factory, it was warm and dry. "Now at the age of 83, and still "lish", [the Cumbrian vernacular for "fit"]. Tommy is arguably the last survivor in the town, of an industry that once employed thousands of people throughout the Lake District.

His tale is worth the telling, for recollections of an industry that produced almost half of the bobbins that were required for the world's textile industry. "Aye we sent them all over the world." said Tommy.

He lived in one of the cottages alongside the mill. "I was only four year old when I went to live down yonder. I went to school from there, an' when you got to 14 , and left school, you got a job in t' factory you see. We lived in t' firm's houses, so that was it. The lads just got any jobs to do, but I was lucky and was taken on as a bobbin turner, and I had to serve my time with that for a lot of years to learn the trade. They only needed so many apprentices so I suppose I was lucky. They used to employ about 120 so it was a big thing for Keswick. It kept Keswick gaan.".

This former industrial site of Low Briery is in a sheltered hollow, and surrounded by trees, much of which is the remainder of formerly coppiced woodland." There'd be a great pile of wood up there, you know, trees, and there'd be big wooden cranes swinging timber on to laal bogeys to run down rails to the saw shed."

"There was plenty of timber already here, but they used to import wood, that timber called teak, but it was mostly local wood d'y know. The wood used to come in green, they had their own wood cutters chopping trees down, and their own wood wagons to bring it in."

In Tommy's early days, these were horse drawn wagons, which were later phased out as traction engines took over to pull the loads. "There was about six different piles of timber and six different cranes , you'd twine a handle down here somewhere, and it lifted a tree up to take it on til a bogey to run it down on rails into the saw mill."

There, the saw machinery which was driven by the power generated by the fast flowing river Greta, would cut the rough timber to size before it went to the drying sheds.

"We called them kilns where the wood went to dry out. It all had to be properly dried before it could be used, then when it was ready, it came into the turning sheds where it was cut into different size bobbins. There was all different machines set up to make the different sizes, it was something like a lathe."

The nearby steam boiler house provided the heat for drying the wood. Tommy explained that in his day, a useful bye product of the drying kilns was gas, which was used on the site to supplement the water power that was diverted by sluices from the river Greta. "In the old days, the whole mill used to be water driven, but then gas and electric took over."

The finished wooden bobbins were then taken to the nearby goods yard of Keswick railway station from where they were transported along the rails of the Cockermouth, Keswick and Penrith Railway, to supply the industrial heartlands of the cotton and woollen industries of Lancashire and Yorkshire.

Tommy explained that there used to be a small station at Low Briery. "Aye the train used to stop here every morning for the workers to get off that had come from Cockermouth or Keswick, then it would be back again at half past five to take them home."

Tommy still has a collection of differently shaped wooden bobbins that show the great variety that were made. Among them is a reel for fishing line. " Aye, we used to make these , then they used to fill them with what was used for fishing line, and sell them. T' others was there for wire, and wool and cotton and whatever was needed. We used to make some that was long enough for carpets to go on. Some of the bobbins was big enough to sit on, like stools you might say."

Tommy worked for the mill when it was owned by Coward Phillipson Co. Keswick, and proudly recalled that although the wage for a time served bobbin turner was £3.1.6 for a 48 hour week, his mill was the first to work a 5 day week in the Keswick area. "And there was no reduction in the wages for the 5 day week. On a Friday night, you queued up, over there. They shouted your number out and you got your pay in a laal tin box."

Bobbin making was not the only industry practised at Low Briery, for in earlier times, a pencil mill utilised the black wad from the Borrowdale mines, and a textile mill made intricate bottom edgings for waistcoats. The latter gave the area its local name, "Aye, they used to call it Fancy Bottom down here," said Tommy, but if that name still lingers, it was the bobbin mill that brought work to the town. At peak production time, the mill at Low Briery turned out 40,000,000 bobbins a year. Even those that held the threads for the coronation gown of Queen Elizabeth 11 were manufactured at Low Briery.

In the last thirty years this former industrial site has become a secluded holiday village and it is hard to imagine the former scene of industrial activity. Tidy stretches of a tar macadam parking area cover what was once the floor of the turning shed that was littered with curled shavings from the spinning blades that shaped the bobbins. The joiners shop has gone, replaced by a new toilet block. "It wasn't like that in my day, we had a board with about four holes spread along it, opening on to the earth. A fella used to come along with a cart and shovel muck over it", Tommy recalled.

The station has disappeared; all that remains is the raised mound of a stone edged platform alongside a public footpath, which has become a popular and attractive walk. Some old photographs and an information board beside the footpath are all that remain to tell the tale. Faded faces below flat cloth caps show unsmiling expressions as they look out from the formal photograph of the work force, where some of the faces were familiar to Tommy ; "This is the ambulance fella, he used to bandage you up when you cut your fingers; I knew quite a few of these. I was nobbut a lad then, and they had been there for a while."

Had he any regrets about its closure, and the changed nature of the site? "Oh dear no," he laughed, "Ivverything's got to mek progress, hasn't it. That's the way of the world".

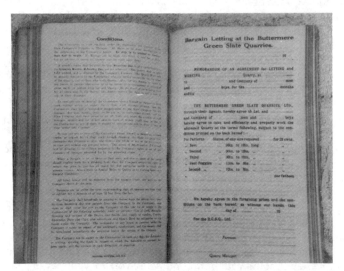

Quarry bargain page

Part of the Honister Quarry workforce, c 1910

Sign at the site of the Low Briery bobbin mill.

*Tommy Richardson at the site of the former railway station
that served the Low Briery bobbin mill.*

CHAPTER FOURTEEN

There's more ways to catch a Fish!

While the lower reaches of the River Derwent hold what is often regarded as some of the best salmon fishing in England, its upper reaches, beyond Grange Bridge, do not hold the same excitement for the angler. Part of the blame must lie with the nature of the river. It is subjected to rapid changes in depth, and ferocity of flow, when a heavy downpour of rain in the mountains can change a peaceful river into a raging torrent. With such conditions, the fertilised eggs of salmon or trout are swept away into the deep water of the lake, where they fall prey to any of the birds, or larger predatory fish.

Derwentwater holds good numbers of fish, but those that are caught are most often pike and perch, with the added nuisance of eels that entangle their slimy bodies round an angler's line. You can sit on one of the launch jetties and watch the striped perch swimming round the shadowed water, while for the youngsters, shoaling minnows give plenty of excitement as they flash and turn silver in an attempt to avoid the jar or net. There are trout in the lake, and also in the upper reaches of the Derwent, where even in the small feeder becks, goodly sized mountain trout can be caught; if not by legitimate means with rod and line, then by the old time skill of tickling. This is an illegal form of catching fish, much practised by poachers. What does "tickling for trout" involve?

First of all, a trout must be spotted, and this can sometimes prove difficult as the coloration of the back of a fish tends to take on the dark colour of underwater, moss covered rocks. Very often the slightest vibration of a foot step on a beck side, or an ill cast shadow can send the fish gliding into the imagined safety of the overhanging bank. Once the hiding place has been marked, the "fisherman" gently slides a hand through the water until the palm, held uppermost is below the fishes belly. A gentle stroking action is almost enough to immobilise the fish, before a swift flicking action scoops it on to the bank.

The Derwent is fed by a number of smaller becks, and it is in these, such as Honister, Langstrath or Styhead where a series of deep pools are to be found. These are interlinked by waterfalls, and quiet shallow stretches where, in some cases, the flow of water barely covers the stones. These becks provide their own fascinating fishing grounds, for it is in the deep pools that the largest of the beck trout lie. The skill of the "fisherman" is to coax these wily creatures into the edge of an accessible bank from where they can be "tickled".

Langstrath Beck has some marvellously deep holes that make superb bathing pools on a hot day, and although these abound with trout, the steep rocky sides of the dubs make it impossible to get a hand on the fish. In such a situation, fish have been known to respond with great alacrity to a hook baited with nothing more than a piece of bread soaked in a savoury spread. But of course, these methods of catching fish although totally illegal, detract nothing from the delicious taste of poached trout, cooked on a hot stone set in the ashes of an open fire, beside the beck where the trout was caught.

Association with "trout" in the valley of Borrowdale can be seen in the name of the side valley of Troutdale. It was here that an early form of fish farming was begun in the

Tales of a Lakeland Valley - BORROWDALE

latter half of the nineteenth century by two men, a Dr Parnaby, and a Mr J J Armistead. A visit to Troutdale today reveals little of the venture, other than the remains of stone tanks sunk into the ground. The trout farm complex consisted of a number of large buildings in which different stages of the fish rearing process were carried out. The hatchery itself was a stone building in which there were trays of fertilised fish eggs. The rearing shed covered the cement lined tanks sunk into the ground which held different sizes of fish. There was a continuous flow of water through the tanks from the small stream in the valley, and from a spring, alongside which the stone tanks were built. Today, only the slate sided outdoor rearing ponds remain.

The purpose of the Troutdale project was not to rear fish for the table, but to sell the small fish to those wishing to restock, or improve rivers, ponds and lakes, mainly for private fishing. Mr Armistead was a great believer in raising a great variety of fish, and could offer for sale, almost thirty different varieties of salmon, trout and char at different stages of development. The hatchery was a great success for about fifteen years, by which time it had become too large a concern to continue in a remote Lakeland valley. Mr Armistead moved to Dumfries to set up a new development, and by 1870, Dr Parnaby was in sole charge at Troutdale.

He was puzzled by the lack of salmon in the upper reaches of the Derwent, and wanted to prove that it was actually possible for a Borrowdale born salmon to return to spawn in the river of its birth. He planned an experiment based at Troutdale. Some fine Derwent salmon in spawning condition were obtained, and the females were stripped of their eggs, which were then fertilised with the milt of the males. These eggs were put into the hatching trays, and after six weeks the small fish that successfully hatched, were large enough to be transferred to the rearing ponds. The fish were carefully reared for over a year, and watched over by Tom Jenkins who was not unknown to repel unwanted visitors with the threats of what he would do to them with his axe.

Alan Mounsey of Grange remembers one encounter. "He was a bit of an eccentric character that was left in charge. He went everywhere carrying a big axe. He came after me one day up there, and I had the presence of mind to say, That's a big fish! He looked down at it, and that gave me the chance to get away."

Dr Parnaby released thousands of yearling fish into the Derwent, most by way of the Troutdale stream, but before they were released, each carried a small tag on a fin just above the tail. They disappeared through the watercourse of the Derwent on their way to sea. For over twelve months there was nothing heard or seen of the fish, and then in 1874, Tom Jenkins rushed to tell Dr Parnaby the great news; he had seen a Troutdale tagged fish lying in a pool between the lake and Grange Bridge. This was the proof that Parnaby had been seeking; it was possible for salmon to come back to the upper reaches of the River Derwent. Natural enthusiasm overtook scientific thought at that stage, for the fish that had travelled thousands of miles was diverted by means of netting barriers in the river, to one of the Troutdale outdoor ponds. Dr Parnaby was so anxious to display the evidence of his successful experiment that the fish was kept in a display tank, where it subsequently died. No opportunity was taken to include that particular fish in any further breeding programme.

It ended up being stuffed, still carrying its Troutdale tag.

Borrrowdale - some useful information

Nearest town;   Keswick

Accommodation;   Hotels, guest houses, self catering accommodation.

Catering;   **Summer;** Cafes at Watendlath,Grange, Stonethwaite, and High Lodore Farm provide a range of snacks and light meals. Licensed restaurant at Seatoller
Bar and evening meals available in many hotels.
Winter; restricted opening.

Tourist Information;   Keswick, 017687 72645

LDNP Information;   Keswick, 017687 72803
Seatoller Barn, 017687 77294

Youth Hostels;   Keswick, 017687 72484
Barrow House, 017687 77246
Longthwaite 017687 77257
Honister Hause, 017687 77267

Camp Sites;   Ashness Farm 017687 77361
Stonethwaite 017687 77234
Seatoller 017687 77284
Hollows Farm, Grange 017687 77298

Car Parking;   National Trust Car Parks at: Great Wood, Ashness, Kettlewell, Bowder Stone, Rosthwaite, Seatoller. [free to members]
Limited free parking available at Grange, Stonethwaite, and Seathwaite.

Public Amenities;   **Toilets;** Grange, Lodore, Bowder Stone, Rosthwaite, Seatoller, Watendlath
Telephone; Grange, Rosthwaite, Stonethwaite, Seatoller , Watendlath

Tales of a Lakeland Valley - BORROWDALE

Public Transport;   Daily service from Keswick to Borrowdale
National Trust weekend minibus service to Watendlath

Boat hire;   Rowing boats, and small motor boats may be hired from
the lakeside landings, Keswick. Motor launches run a
regular service round the lake. Limited winter service.

Petrol;   There are no facilities for buying petrol in Borrowdale.
Fill up in Keswick.

Shopping;   The village store at Rosthwaite has a wide range of goods.

Post Office;   Stonethwaite.

Guided walks;   These leave the Moot Hall at Keswick every day.
Details available from information centres.

Mountain Rescue;   New headquarters will be at Lake Road Car park,
Keswick, from 1996.
Ring 999 in case of emergency

Police;   Keswick 01900 602422

Hospital;   Cottage hospital facilities at Keswick 017687 72012
Major casualty hospitals - West Cumberland Hospital.
Whitehaven 01946 693181
Cumberland Infirmary, Carlisle

Churches;   St. Kentigern C/E, Crosthwaite, Keswick
St. John C/E, Keswick.
St. Andrew C/E, Rosthwaite
Holy Trinity, C/E, Grange in Borrowdale
Our Lady of the Lake and St.. Charles, RC, Keswick
Methodist Church, Keswick
Methodist Chapel, Grange in Borrowdale.

Showtime
Borrowdale Show

This is a traditional valley show

Date;   Third Sunday in September 10am - 5pm

Venue;   **Rosthwaite**

Programme includes;   **Morning;**   Judging of Herdwick and Swaledale sheep.
                                          Judging of hounds, fell ponies.
                                          Sheep dog trials
                          Afternoon; Cumberland and Westmorland wrestling.
                                          Fell races. Hound trailing. Stick judging.
                                          Parade of fox hounds. Sheep shearing.
                                          Tug of war. Vintage vehicles and machinery.
                                          All entries taken on field

On field facilities;   Craft tent
                                          Variety of trade and display stands
                                          Catering
                                          Beer Tent
                                          Toilets

Car Parking;   In field alongside main valley road.
                                          Limited disabled parking on show field
                                          Contact the Show Secretary 017687 - 77678
                                          to pre-book a space

Borrowdale Showfield as seen from the Watendlath track.

Crowds gather at the end of the Senior Fell Race.

Bibliography

History and Directory of Cumberland - Bulmer 1901
History and Directory of West Cumbria - Bulmer 1883
Cummerland Talk - John Richardson
Observations chiefly relative to the Picturesque Beauty....
particularly the Mountains and Lakes of Cumberland
and Westmorland - W. Gilpin. 1772
The History of Cumberland - Wm Hutchinson
Iron Ores - Bernard Smith
Landscape and Society in Medieval Cumbria - Angus Winchester
Lake District History - W G Collingwood

To the best of the author's knowledge, all information is correct at the time of going to press

River Derwent at Grange in Borrowdale